The Keys to Mentoring Success

KATHY WENTWORTH DRAHOSZ

ISBN 0-9748859-0-8

DEDICATIONS

TO MY HUSBAND, Jurij Drahosz, who has been my champion and confidant. His constant support and encouragement has given me the confidence to accomplish my personal and professional goals.

TO MY MOTHER, Barbara Burns Fife, who taught me how to believe in myself, love unconditionally and enjoy life!

ACKNOWLEDGEMENTS

There have been many key people who have made wonderful contributions to this book, but several deserve special recognition:

Jennifer Cunningham, my Vice President of Business Operations, who helped me to stay true to my goals and dreams. Over the past several years she has managed the day-to-day client relations and business operations so that I could dedicate my time and energy into creating and finalizing this book.

Trisha Milligan, my Executive Assistant, who helped to keep the office running smoothly and professionally. Her quick wit and great sense of humor brings a welcomed playfulness to the office.

Alison Sfreddo, my Editor, who has a magical way with words. She helped me capture the key points in this book in a way that has made it easier for the reader to follow and understand and at the same time kept my own true voice.

Leslie Williams, my Executive Coach and Editor, for helping to shape the flow and content of this book.

Katherine Drahosz for helping me to balance the multiple demands of career and home.

Mimi Eanes for her creativity and exceptional graphic design.

Jo Ann Vaught, who challenged me 18 years ago to design a training program that showed people how to find and cultivate successful mentoring relationships. Jo Ann's challenge helped me to find my life's work; my calling.

Thank you to the following special people for taking the time to read advance copies of this book and for providing your valuable feedback, support and encouragement: Tony Cunningham, Diane Dixon, Doug Evans, Barbara Fife, Linda Matheny, Jan Northup, Jennifer Sinek, Jo Ann Vaught, Tiffany Shemory, and Joyce Smith.

ACKNOWLEDGEMENTS

Thank you to those who have shown me the value of mentoring, my mentors

Edwin William Wentworth • Barbara Fife • Linda Matheny • Milton Mallett • Diane Dixon • Carol Earle • Denise Bradshaw • Ken Harris • John V. Kerr • Sam Romano • Butch Wentworth • Ron Petrie • Jan Northup • Bonnie Wasmund • Kevin Kirby • Earl Fife • Jo Ann Vaught • Jurij Drahosz • Joyce Smith • Janet Vitalis • Vera Fletcher • Diane Rhodes • Margo Murray • Sharon Jenks • Heather Brown • Bill Bonnstetter • Sandi Strohmeier • Rollie Waters • David Matthews • Luba Drahosz • Elaine Kontos • Paula Boyd • Jim Matheny • Debbie Young • Chris Emond • Kathleen Allenbaugh • Ed Jenks • Katherine Drahosz • Ann Hibbard • Marty Herrin • Karen Weller • Jennifer Cunningham • Doug Evans • Tiffany Shemory • Leslie Williams • Dave Schoof • Jennifer Sinek • Nichole Richmond • Sherry Sherman • Lloyd Raines • Kevin Whittaker • Randy Plasse • Chris Orsini • Anne Cregger • Trisha Milligan • Bob Hickman • Chris Shemory • Alison Sfreddo • Skip Pettit • Kanu Kogod • Adam Cunningham

"If I have been able to see further than others,
it is because I stood on the shoulders of giants."

Sir Isaac Newton

CONTENTS

1

Introduction to Mentoring

IF THIS BOOK has found its way into your hands, then you must be a *people developer.* People development is an awesome, demanding and rewarding job. When you look back on your career there will be very few opportunities when you can honestly say, "*I made a difference,*" unless you are taking the time to develop others. ***The Keys to Mentoring Success*** is based on the fundamental principle that people learn best from other people.

In a survey conducted by Dr. Jan Northup on what has had the most impact on an individual's career development, employees consistently identified the guidance and support of a mentor as a key factor in their success (Northup, 1988). However, developing people does not stop with access to a supportive mentor; people need to be at the right place at the right time. In addition, they need a variety of developmental experiences that give them a broader view of the organization and its formal and informal structures. They also need a network of professional contacts that help them gain access and exposure to people at all levels within the organization. Most importantly, they need the opportunity to showcase their potential.

I believe there is a lot of untapped talent buried in our organizations today, and for whatever reason, these people have not been given the opportunity to demonstrate their potential and value to the organization. The most successful "people developers" understand this and consciously create richly diverse opportunities for employees to learn and showcase their value to the organization.

THE BOTTOM LINE

With decades of experience in assisting organizations in the establishment of formal and informal mentoring programs, my colleagues and I have built a unique and systematic approach to people development. **The Mentoring Connection©** has become a benchmark in human resource development and has changed the lives of thousands. It is the model we will explore in this book.

The purpose of this book is to provide organizations with a detailed roadmap for implementing their own formal mentoring connections. Practitioners will explore, in depth, the principles and processes for planning, designing and executing a successful mentoring program within their organization. Each chapter will end with **PRACTICAL EXAMPLES AND TECHNIQUES** which will illustrate how the concepts presented can be applied.

WHY IS MENTORING IMPORTANT?

Mentoring is a time-honored tradition that has revolutionized the way people develop. Organizations worldwide are realizing the value of mentoring and are investing time, money and resources into facilitating successful developmental mentoring relationships. Why has mentoring made such a comeback? The answer is simple; it is a valuable and cost effective tool for developing people.

Many of the most successful public and private organizations are those that have come to the realization that investing in their own people will reap the biggest returns. Organizations worldwide have implemented innovative and dynamic mentoring programs. These professional partnerships have not only proved to boost morale within the organization, but have also increased productivity and efficiency.

Mentoring, rich in history and tradition, has made a resurgence in the twenty-first century as a result of four key factors:

1. **Massive Change.** To compete successfully in today's work environment, organizations need employees who can deal effectively with change. Mentors can provide valuable insight, guidance and continuity in a changing work environment. They can also help employees envision a broader perspective of the organization's mission, direction and future. More importantly, they share timely

information so employees can position themselves with the skills necessary for success.

Mentoring reaps another, often unexpected, benefit in times of change—it keeps the mentors learning as well. Mentoring is a way to keep seasoned leaders current for "teaching is the best teacher."

2. New Employee-Employer Relationship. Today's work environment has created a new employee-employer relationship. Employees can no longer look to the organization for long-term job security. They must learn how to position themselves for long-term employability (Waterman, Waterman & Collard, 1994). Long-term employability means no longer thinking of oneself as a job description, but rather as a package of marketable skills that can be transferred from one job to the next when there is no longer a win-win for the organization and the employee. Mentoring fits well in this culture. It helps employees position themselves with the right people, the right skills and the right work environment.

3. Technological Advancements. Communication technology (e-mail, voice mail, fax machine) has changed the way people communicate. People can go for days without talking to a real person. Although technology has revolutionized the way we stay connected, it has, in fact, hindered our ability to build personal and professional relationships. Mentoring reaffirms the value of the "human connection."

4. An Aging Workforce. Throughout history, leaders have been responsible for passing along the wisdom of experience from one generation to the next. As the 21st century progresses, thousands of employees will be ready for retirement (Bureau of Labor Statistics). This critical depletion of experienced and seasoned workers has forced employers to rethink the methods used to develop future leaders and to ensure that institutional knowledge does not vanish with its retiring workers. Traditional succession plans and antiquated training approaches are no longer keeping pace. Mentoring offers an efficient process of cultivating the next generation of leaders.

Mentoring is a valuable developmental tool that has become an integral part of today's rapidly changing business world. Today's employers are investing time, energy and resources in developing productive and fulfilled employees. Mentoring is an effective strategy for retaining organizational wisdom, producing tomorrow's leaders and cultivating organizational agility.

WHAT IS MENTORING?

In its simplest form, mentoring is people helping people grow and develop. It is the process of transferring knowledge from one individual to another. The mentoring relationship can take many forms and is always driven by the needs of the organization and the learning goals of the employee. The most common types of mentoring are outlined below:

Supervisory Mentoring. Supervisory mentors share valuable information about the organization and provide meaningful work and developmental learning opportunities to their direct reports. They expose employees to the values of the organization (i.e., who and what gets rewarded or punished) and can help employees position themselves with the skills necessary for success.

Situational Mentoring. Situational mentoring is, in essence, *the right help at the right time* (Drahosz & Rhodes, 1997). It is a spontaneous connection (whether it be a brief introduction at a conference, on an airplane or in a business meeting) that can help someone solve a problem or encourage them to uncover a hidden talent.

Informal Mentoring. Informal mentoring is the type of mentoring connection most people can relate to and have most likely experienced. It is an informal relationship built

SITUATIONAL MENTORING

Don Shula and Ken Blanchard (1995) describe situational mentoring in their book *Everyone's a Coach:*

> "One entry point, one teachable moment presents itself, and you step in. It may happen in a conversation with a neighbor's child or a friend's relative or an employee of someone else that you plant the seed. When something draws you to a person, trust that feeling. You may be creating a turning point in that person's life."

on mutual trust and respect. An employee sees a quality in another person that they admire and would like to develop; or a mentor sees something in another person that reminds him of himself. Informal mentoring relationships are generally nurtured over a long period of time and sometimes last the length of a person's career (Drahosz & Rhodes, 1997).

Informal mentors open new doors, share valuable lessons and expose people to information and experiences to which they would not normally have access in the day-to-day responsibilities of their assigned jobs.

Formal Mentoring. A formal mentoring partnership is a carefully constructed learning relationship. Its formal support is comprehensive and includes a facilitated matching process, formal training and clear goals for measuring success. Formal mentoring is very attractive to most organizations because it develops individual employees while simultaneously strengthening the overall organization. This book focuses on building and cultivating **formal** mentoring connections.

NOTES

NOTES

2

Establish a Program Support Structure

THE MULTI-DIMENSIONAL NATURE of a formal mentoring program requires a strong internal support system. This internal support system consists of three critical roles: Program Champion (Sponsor), Program Coordinator and Mentoring Design Team.

THE ROLE OF THE PROGRAM CHAMPION

For a formal mentoring program to succeed in the short and long term, it will need a Program Champion. A well-respected senior leader, who believes mentoring is a valuable tool for employee development, can bring both enthusiasm and credibility to the program. The Program Champion commissions the formal program, sells it to other senior leaders within the organization, removes roadblocks and secures (or advocates for) the necessary funding. Whenever possible, Program Champions are also involved as mentors and are willing to make presentations at key junctures in the program. In other words, they remain a visible presence throughout the entire mentoring process. The responsibilities of the Program Champion are as follows:

- Collaborates with Program Coordinator in identifying and recruiting mentors.
- Provides guidance and periodically attends meetings

with the Mentoring Design Team.

- Informs management of key program highlights.
- Removes organizational obstacles to the program's success.
- Participates in the program as a mentor.
- Serves as management liaison between the mentoring Program Coordinator and senior management.
- Officially kicks off the mentoring program.
- Assists the Program Coordinator in the marketing of the mentoring program by providing endorsement letters and testimonials for inclusion in outgoing correspondence.
- Assists the Program Coordinator with program enhancements.

THE ROLE OF THE PROGRAM COORDINATOR

The Program Coordinator is responsible for synchronizing and coordinating the various elements of the formal mentoring program. The Program Coordinator is the focal point for carrying out the overall program goals and will serve as the point of contact for senior management as well as for the mentors and mentorees. The Program Coordinator will also serve as a resource for participants by helping them to develop personalized mentoring activities, while at the same time measuring progress and troubleshooting problems.

A dedicated Program Coordinator works in harmony with the various external mentoring Consultants involved in supporting the mentoring program. Often, the Program Coordinator will share the platform at kickoff sessions, orientations and at various training programs, and contribute their first-hand knowledge, credibility and influence to help the program succeed. The responsibilities of the Program Coordinator are as follows:

- Provides support, funding and accountability for the mentoring program.
- Ensures completion of planned benchmarks, project evaluations, and reporting.
- Coordinates the logistics (room, equipment, speakers) for the various training programs, panels and workshops.
- Troubleshoots problems that arise in the partnerships or with supervisors regarding participation in the program.
- Coordinates internal and external project communications.
- Facilitates the design and distribution of promotional mentoring program material. (This may include working with the Mentoring Design Team to ensure that all team members are aware of recruitment efforts.)
- Coordinates recruitment, selection, and matching of

mentorees and mentors. (This may include providing feedback to mentors and mentorees regarding why they were not selected for the mentoring program.)

THE ROLE OF THE MENTORING DESIGN TEAM

The mentoring process also requires sponsorship throughout the organization and support that transcends all functions and levels. Without the support and guidance of credible advocates, even the best-designed programs may flounder. Establishing a Mentoring Design Team that will guide, promote and lend credibility to the program will be one of the most significant tasks in getting a program off the ground. The Mentoring Design Team is a group of dedicated, credible volunteers who bring a variety of perspectives and viewpoints to the program. This team plays a vital role in designing, marketing and shaping the direction of future mentoring programs. The responsibilities of the Mentoring Design Team are as follows:

- Designs and establishes the goals for the program (with the Program Champion's input and approval) and works in tandem with the Program Coordinator in determining how the program will be constructed and executed.
- Markets the program through formal briefings and

informal networking and advocacy.

- Oversees the distribution of mentoring program promotional materials and information within circles of influence.
- Assists the Program Coordinator in recruitment and selection.
- Provides guidance and advice to the Program Coordinator, as necessary, to resolve problems.
- Reviews all program evaluations and approves final reports.
- Determines the direction of future programs.

EXTERNAL MENTORING CONSULTANTS

Another optional support role is that of an external Consultant. Many model programs create partnerships with private Consultants to help guide internal Program Coordinators in the planning, implementing and continual evaluation of the program. Experienced outside Consultants lend knowledge and experience to the mentoring process and provide an objective viewpoint. The private Consultant often serves as a confidential process advisor for both the Mentoring Design Team and the mentoring partnerships.

TECHNOLOGY AS A PROGRAM COORDINATION TOOL

A number of mentoring Program Coordinators are now using the Internet to streamline and manage the administrative processes required of formal mentoring programs. **The Mentoring Connection©** offers innovative web-based tools to help facilitate program logistics while maintaining the personal aspects critical to effective mentoring programs. (See Appendix A for details.)

SUMMARY

Once you have gained the internal support structures necessary to establish and shape the program, it is time to begin creating your mentoring program. Chapter 3 serves as a Quick User's Guide, as it provides a snapshot of ***The Keys to Mentoring Success.*** Chapters 4-10 will walk you through the entire seven-step Mentoring Connection process; from initial planning, through implementation, to the final stage of program evaluation.

PRACTICAL EXAMPLES AND TECHNIQUES

In both the public and private sectors, organizations are using in-house design teams to build their mentoring programs and are realizing significant benefits. To highlight some examples:

- **US CUSTOMS SERVICE (USCS), SAIC NEW ORLEANS**
  The USCS 10 member Leadership Development Council includes senior agents from both the field and regional headquarters. The team provided direction and active support for the formal mentoring program. In addition, senior agents served as mentors, presenters and facilitators during the year long process. (USCS, SAIC, 1999).

- **US VETERANS HEALTH ADMINISTRATION (VHA)**
  VHA employee development programs are guided by an internal Leadership Development Council. Senior leaders throughout the organization serve as mentors in the program and conduct round table discussion groups at various points in the program (VHA, 2001).

- **NASA GODDARD**
  At NASA Goddard, employee development is one of the Director's main initiatives supporting a high performance work environment (Strategic Implementation Plan, 2003). Senior leaders support the Director's commitment by championing the mentoring process, which, in turn, ensures the program's credibility. The Mentoring Design Team is made up of professionals from the entire organization and represents several career fields. The team plays an active role in supporting the mentoring process from selection of the candidates to the matching and training of participants. (GSFS, 2003).

As illustrated in the examples on page 17, the involvement of a team of dedicated stakeholders creates both support and visibility for the programs. Not only do they help to build the process, but they are also active participants. Be sure to select team members (approximately 6-8) who bring different points of view to the table. For example, consider including the following in your design team:

- a Program Coordinator
- a Potential Mentor
- a Potential Mentoree
- a Manager
- a Human Resource Development Specialist
- a Public Relations Specialist
- a Union Representative (if appropriate)

Roles and Responsibilities

Provide team members with a framework of their roles and responsibilities to help them to better understand the value they bring to the team. Identify the roles and responsibilities of Program Champion, Program Coordinator and Mentoring Design Team:

PROGRAM CHAMPION: ____________________

____

____

____

PROGRAM COORDINATOR(s): ______________

____

____

____

MENTORING DESIGN TEAM: ______________

____

____

____

3

The Mentoring Connection: An overview

CORE DESIGN PRINCIPLES

The Mentoring Connection (TMC) is a comprehensive, systematic approach to formal mentoring. Implemented in scores of private and public organizations, **The Mentoring Connection** has a highly successful track record for helping individuals grow while enabling organizations to meet strategic goals. **The Mentoring Connection** is based upon the seven core design principles (found in Table 1) that function together to create a strong, highly effective, and sustainable mentoring program.

TABLE 1: THE MENTORING CONNECTION'S CORE DESIGN PRINCIPLES

Relevance: Programs are designed specifically to meet the unique requirements of the organization and its employees.

Top management support: Senior leaders recognize the importance of the mentoring program and visibly demonstrate their support through their words, actions and resources over the short and long term.

Systematic matching: Carefully constructed processes are used to select and match mentors and mentorees.

Role clarity: Mentors' and mentorees' roles and responsibilities are clearly defined and mutually agreed upon.

Variety: Mentorees experience a wide range of learning activities and environments.

Technology: Mentors and mentorees use the Internet to streamline and manage the administrative details of their mentoring partnerships.

Evaluation: Processes are implemented to continually evaluate and refine the program and its components.

7 STEPS TO MENTORING SUCCESS

The Mentoring Connection process serves as a model to help you design and implement a successful formal mentoring program that is customized to meet your organization's unique needs and culture. The strategies for building a formal mentoring program are the same whether you are designing a program for six partnerships or sixty.

The Mentoring Connection Process:

STEP 1: Plan the program's purpose and design.

STEP 2: Identify potential mentors and mentorees.

STEP 3: Facilitate a joint orientation that includes mentors, mentorees, and supervisors.

STEP 4: Match mentors and mentorees.

STEP 5: Provide mentoring training and tools.

STEP 6: Implement Mentoring Action Plans and Mentoring Agreements.

STEP 7: Evaluate and track progress and redesign as necessary (Return to Step 1).

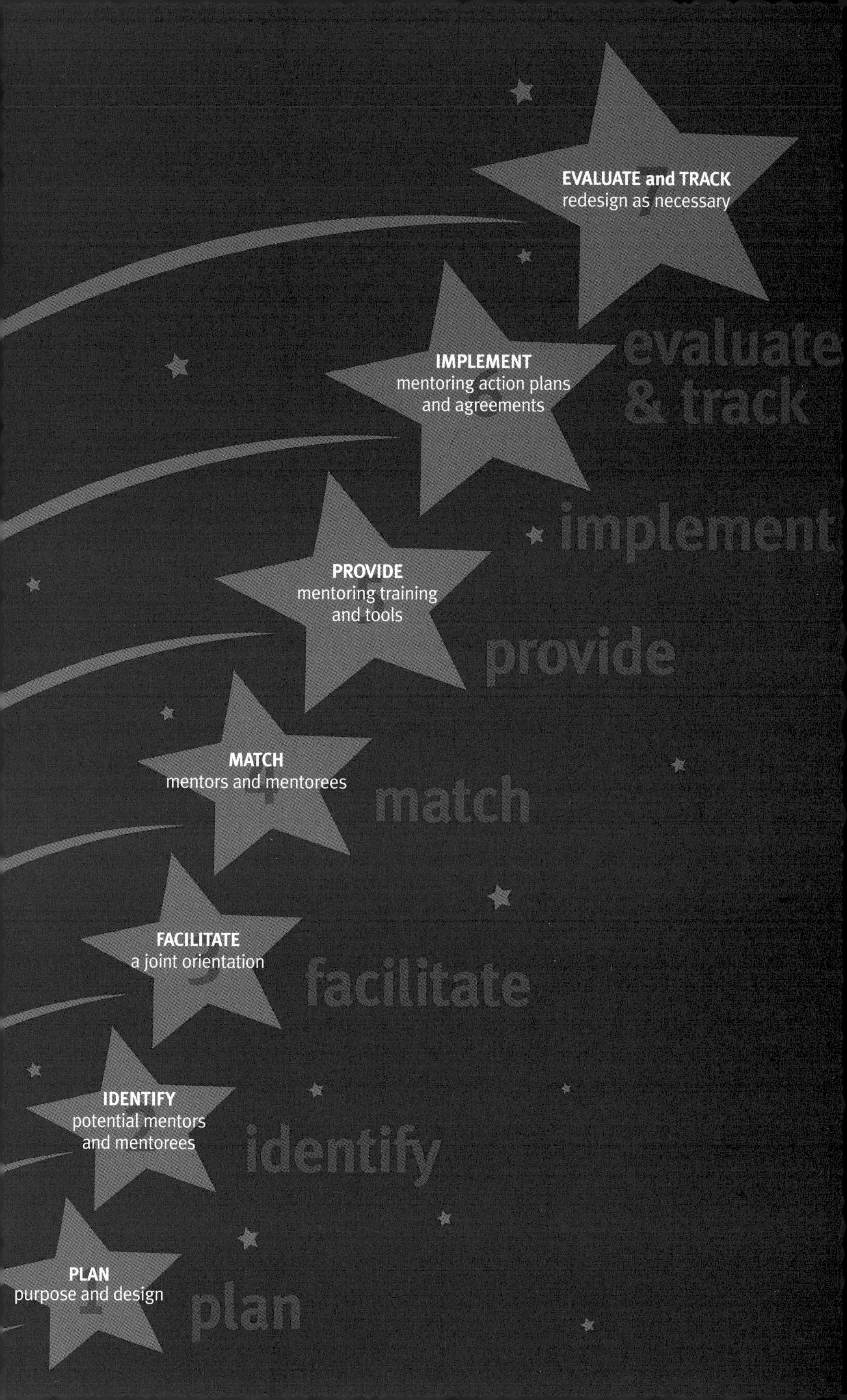

EVALUATE and TRACK
redesign as necessary

7

evaluate & track

IMPLEMENT
mentoring action plans and agreements

6

implement

PROVIDE
mentoring training and tools

5

provide

MATCH
mentors and mentorees

4

match

FACILITATE
a joint orientation

3

facilitate

IDENTIFY
potential mentors and mentorees

2

identify

PLAN
purpose and design

1

plan

STEP 1: Plan the Program's Purpose and Design.

A carefully-selected group of stakeholders (the Mentoring Design Team) will meet to design and develop program objectives, guidelines and action plans based on the specific needs of the organization. The Mentoring Design Team produces a Mentoring Plan which outlines the sequence of events necessary to implement the program. The Mentoring Plan also addresses how the organization will approach each of The Mentoring Connection's core design principles as described in Table 1, and as such, will need to answer the following questions:

- How can mentoring help the organization meet its strategic goals?
- How will top management support be achieved?
- How will mentors and mentorees be selected and matched?
- What will be expected of mentors and mentorees?
- What learning experiences will be available to participants?
- How will the overall program be evaluated and refined?

The Mentoring Plan also identifies the program support structure and outlines the roles and responsibilities of a Program Champion, Program Coordinator and the Mentoring Design Team.

TMC CORE DESIGN PRINCIPLES: Step 1 covers all of the TMC design principles with emphasis on Relevance and Top Management Support

STEP 2: Identify Potential Mentors and Mentorees.

The success of any mentoring program depends on the careful recruitment and selection of mentors and mentorees. Using specific criteria developed in the program design (Step 1), the Program Coordinator and Mentoring Design Team will recruit volunteers to participate as mentors and identify mentoree candidates.

TMC CORE DESIGN PRINCIPLES: Relevance, Role Clarity, Technology

STEP 3: Facilitate a Joint Mentor-Mentoree-Supervisor Orientation.

Sponsoring a joint orientation workshop will help mentors, mentorees and supervisors understand both the concept and process of mentoring. A joint orientation will include information about the history of the program; its goals, roles, responsibilities and program support structure. In addition, the orientation will explain the matching process and offer participants specific characteristics to look for in a mentor or mentoree.

TMC CORE DESIGN PRINCIPLES: Top Management Support, Systematic Matching, Role Clarity

STEP 4: Match Mentors and Mentorees.

The Program Coordinator and Mentoring Design Team will implement the matching process that was designed at the program's outset. Every effort will be made to match mentorees with mentors who can best support their developmental needs.

TMC CORE DESIGN PRINCIPLES: Systematic Matching, Technology

STEP 5: Provide Training for Mentoring Program Participants.

A great way to kick off a formal program is with a two-day workshop that will give mentors and mentorees the training and tools they need to engage in successful mentoring relationships. This workshop will provide mentors with the right mix of coaching skills that will help them to share their wisdom and experience. Mentorees will also receive training which will enable them to take advantage of this mentoring opportunity and will encourage them to assume an active role in the advancement of their careers. This workshop marks the official beginning of the formal mentoring relationship. Early products of this session should be a Mentoring Agreement, (which will set the parameters for the mentoring partnership), and a Mentoring Action Plan, (which outlines the mentoree's learning goals and activities).

TMC CORE DESIGN PRINCIPLE: Role Clarity

STEP 6: Implement the Mentoring Process.

Mentors and mentorees will implement their Mentoring Agreements and Mentoring Action Plans. Learning activities usually include both classroom training as well as more experiential activities such as special projects and shadowing experiences. It is recommended that the Program Coordinator check on the mentoring partnerships throughout the year by providing periodic progress reviews, mentoring forums and one-on-one personal contacts.

TMC CORE DESIGN PRINCIPLES: Variety, Evaluation

STEP 7: Evaluate and Track Progress.

There is great benefit in having mentors and mentorees participate in two progress reviews; one at mid-point and one at the end of the program. These reviews give participants the opportunity to ask questions and share their challenges and success stories. This valuable feedback also allows the Program Coordinator to make any mid-point or program-end adjustments that will enhance current or future programs.

TMC CORE DESIGN PRINCIPLE: Evaluation

PRACTICAL EXAMPLES AND TECHNIQUES

Planning for Obstacles

It is important to uncover any potential obstacles or roadblocks in the mentoring program and transform those obstacles into opportunities. Identify any potential hurdles that could cause problems later on:

POTENTIAL OBSTACLE	SOLUTION OR OPPORTUNITY
• Supervisor "buy-in."	• Supervisor involvement early on in the mentoring process.
______________________	______________________
______________________	______________________
______________________	______________________
______________________	______________________
______________________	______________________
______________________	______________________
______________________	______________________
______________________	______________________
______________________	______________________
______________________	______________________

NOTES

4

Plan the Program Purpose Design

STEP 1

THOUGHTFUL PLANNING IS THE KEY to a successful formal mentoring program. Programs with the greatest impact and longevity have been the ones built upon a thorough process of objective setting and design. The program purpose and design process consist of the following components:

- Setting program objectives that are relevant to organizational needs.
- Targeting key skills for development.
- Identifying the mentoring program learning experiences.

SETTING PROGRAM OBJECTIVES THAT ARE RELEVANT TO ORGANIZATIONAL NEEDS

A necessary factor in any successful mentoring program is top management support. Acquiring this vital support proves to the organization that the program is relevant to the needs of the organization as a whole, as well as to the individual participants. Therefore, the design of the mentoring process must be driven by both individual and organizational needs. A program's purpose will **drive** the program goals which will, in turn, **drive** its design.

EXAMPLES OF PROGRAM DESIGNS BASED ON ORGANIZATIONAL OBJECTIVES

The following are examples of mentoring programs based on different organizational needs.

Example 1: A career development mentoring program

PURPOSE: INCREASE JOB SATISFACTION AND JOB FIT

Organizational Goals ··· Drive	Individual Goals ··· Drive	Mentoring Design
• Foster an open environment where information is shared and knowledge is transferred. • Improve individual performance, productivity and innovation. • Increase organizational commitment. • Improve organizational communication.	• Take responsibility for individual career development. • Assess skills and values. • Gain a broader view of the organization. • Grow personally and professionally through challenging assignments and experiences. • Develop important working relationships.	• Mentors who can share information about career development strategies, organizational philosophy and unwritten rules. • Insightful feedback (self, supervisor and/or peers). • Shadowing experiences. • Developmental assignments.

Example 1 illustrates a career development mentoring program designed to increase employee job satisfaction by teaching the employee how to take responsibility for his/her own career development.

Example 2: A new employee orientation mentoring program

PURPOSE: INTEGRATE NEW EMPLOYEES INTO THE ORGANIZATION		
Organizational Goals ···› Drive	**Individual Goals ···› Drive**	**Mentoring Design**
• Attract and retain new employees. • Ensure new employees understand the core skills, values and behaviors expected for success. • Reduce turnover.	• Learn the mission and structure of the organization. • Provide personal support during career transition. • Increase confidence.	• Formal orientation, classroom and on-the-job training. • Mentors who can link classroom training to the workplace. • Mentors who can share information about organizational philosophy and unwritten rules. • Shadowing experiences. • Self-assessment.

Example 2 shows a different type of mentoring program which focuses on attracting new employees to the organization and retaining them. It also ensures that they acquire the appropriate skills for enhanced on-the-job performance.

Example 3: A leadership development mentoring program

PURPOSE: DEVELOP A FUTURE POOL OF LEADERS		
Organizational Goals ⇢ Drive	**Individual Goals ⇢ Drive**	**Mentoring Design**
• Develop a future pool of leaders who have the skills to move to greater responsibility. • Clone corporate knowledge. • Succession planning.	• Develop technical as well as interpersonal skills. • Grow personally and professionally through challenging assignments and experiences. • Develop a better understanding of how the organization conducts business. • Develop important relationships and contacts both internally and externally.	• Challenging assignments that highlight a new skill. • Exposure to senior level meetings. • Senior level mentors who share strategies for balancing technical, interpersonal and political savvy skills. • Multi-rater assessment and feedback.

This last scenario *(Example 3)* explores a mentoring program designed to develop leaders and aid in succession planning. The goal is to position leaders with the complex skills and perspectives that are necessary in positions of greater responsibility.

Each of these examples illustrates the vital link between the program's purpose, goals and the mentoring design. These programs are strong and successful because they simultaneously keep their workforce learning and address important organizational needs.

TARGETING THE SKILLS FOR DEVELOPMENT

Through a series of conversations, the Mentoring Design Team discusses the skills, values and behaviors they perceive as critical for success, both now and in the future. However, there can be a drawback with this process in that there is a risk of building a program based on incorrect perceptions of what success looks like. Rather than producing an objective analysis of the key skills and traits necessary for success, the team may unconsciously create a list of behaviors that describe themselves and fail to distinguish between job effectiveness or ineffectiveness (Dalton & Hollenbeck, 1996).

There are consulting firms that specialize in competency model development and can be an option if the Mentoring

Design Team is concerned about objectivity. The difficulty with this approach is that it can be very time consuming and expensive.

To get the best results, consider using an existing competency model (one that has a proven track record) and have the Mentoring Design Team validate the accuracy of the model within the organization's culture and environment. Look for a model that fits the organization's developmental needs.

EXAMPLES OF COMPETENCY MODELS CURRENTLY AVAILABLE IN THE MARKETPLACE

Benchmarks®, Center for Creative Leadership (CCL)

Leadership Effectiveness Inventory (LEI), Graduate School, USDA

The Success Triangle©, The Training Connection, Inc.

The Success Triangle©

A user-friendly competency model used by a number of public and private organizations is The Success Triangle (Drahosz & Rhodes, 1997). The goal of The Success Triangle is to help mentorees understand the skills, values and behaviors that impact their success on-the-job. The Success Triangle is organized into three-skill areas:

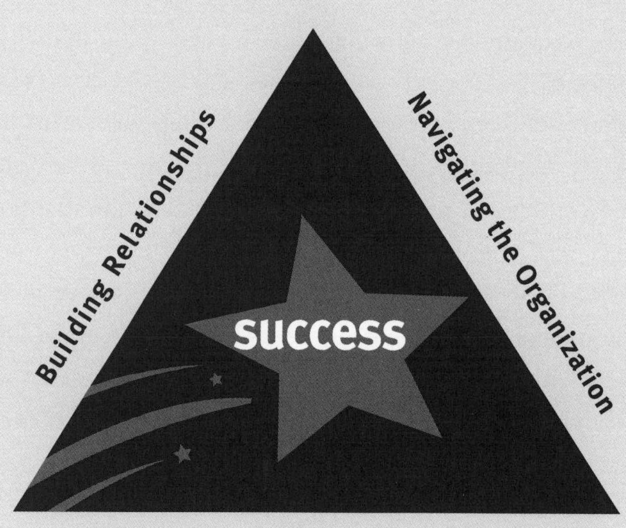

The Success Triangle

1. Expertise – how effective an individual is at mastering the expertise required of their job or career field.

2. Building Relationships – how effective the individual is at building relationships and connections with others.

3. Navigating the Organization – how effective the individual is at understanding and navigating the organization through its formal and informal structures.

We can all think of someone who has great technical ability, intensity, and focused work habits. We might have even referred to them as being bright or incredibly talented technically; but put them in a team environment and they are at a loss. They don't understand the political ramifications of their actions or how their behavior impacts their performance. Their shyness may be perceived as possessive with information and their intensity may be perceived as hard to work with. Without "relationship skills" and "political savvy" a bright, technically oriented employee may not be perceived as an asset to the organization.

By understanding what success looks like and evaluating one's own Success Triangle, mentorees can broaden their competencies and balance their technical skills with complementary interpersonal skills and political savvy.

IDENTIFYING LEARNING EXPERIENCES

A central task of the Mentoring Design Team is to determine the types of learning experiences that will comprise the mentoring program. The team will want to design experiences at two levels: group and individual. The group level experiences will be the core learning activities that all participants will attend throughout the program. The individual level experiences will be a selection of developmental opportunities for the mentorees to choose from that will satisfy their individual learning needs and goals.

GROUP LEARNING EXPERIENCES

Although "structured" by design, the group learning experiences and activities will create "official" support of the program and will promote enthusiasm among its participants. This structure consists of the following components:

Participant Orientation

This session will acquaint the selected mentors, mentorees and the mentorees' supervisors with the goals and benefits of mentoring and explains how the program is structured. The orientation takes place before the formal start of the program and allows participants an opportunity to:

- Meet each other.
- Gain a sense of program expectations.
- Finalize their decision about participating in the program.
- Identify and select a mentoring partner.

Dynamic Mentoring Workshop

Once mentors and mentorees have been matched, it will be important to provide formal mentoring training. The most effective mentoring training programs foster an environment for partners to:

- Build trust and rapport.
- Clarify mentoring roles and responsibilities.
- Address mentoring plans and agreements.

The Dynamic Mentoring Workshop engages participants in a series of career development discussions that will allow time to plan, practice, and apply mentoring skills immediately to the relationship.

Structured Mentoring Forums

Many successful mentoring programs provide periodic classes, or forums, as a part of their mentoring design. These forums give mentors and mentorees a chance to explore timely topics and to exchange ideas and information. The mentoring forums are most

STRUCTURED MENTORING FORUMS

When participants in a formal leadership development program were asked what aspects of the program made the greatest impact, they responded:

- "All of the quarterly forums have been fabulous. As supervisors, we never get enough training."
- "The forums were tremendous. All supervisors should have this opportunity (especially to enhance people skills)."
- "The quarterly forum topics of discussion were outstanding and very beneficial."

effective when the content is based on the mentorees' own interest in the topics.

Mid-Point Energizer Workshop

The mid-point energizer brings mentors and mentorees together to reflect on their learning experiences at the mid-point of the program and makes any necessary adjustments for the remainder of their time together. As part of the mid-point process, the Mentoring Design Team may also construct a way for participants to engage in a written program evaluation. (See Chapter 10 for details on program evaluation).

The mid-point energizer gives participants an opportunity to assess how well the program is working as a whole and how far their individual partnerships are progressing. Armed with this valuable information, the Program Coordinator can make adjustments to the program and the individual mentoring partners can make any helpful course corrections to both their goals and relationships.

End of Program Celebration and Evaluation

The ending of the program should be as carefully designed as its beginning. It is very beneficial to provide mentors and mentorees with a structured opportunity to celebrate their accomplishments during the program and to wrap up their formal partnerships. As part of the program-conclusion process, the Mentoring Design Team should create a method for evaluating the mentoring process from both a programmatic and individual perspective. (See Chapter 10 for more information).

INDIVIDUAL LEARNING EXPERIENCES

The model below illustrates a dynamic mentoring process. This process has many interlocking developmental activities that are supported by an active mentoring experience. In other words, the dynamic mentoring process takes the relationship beyond the philosophical chats with the mentor and looks for developmental opportunities in a variety of situations and learning experiences.

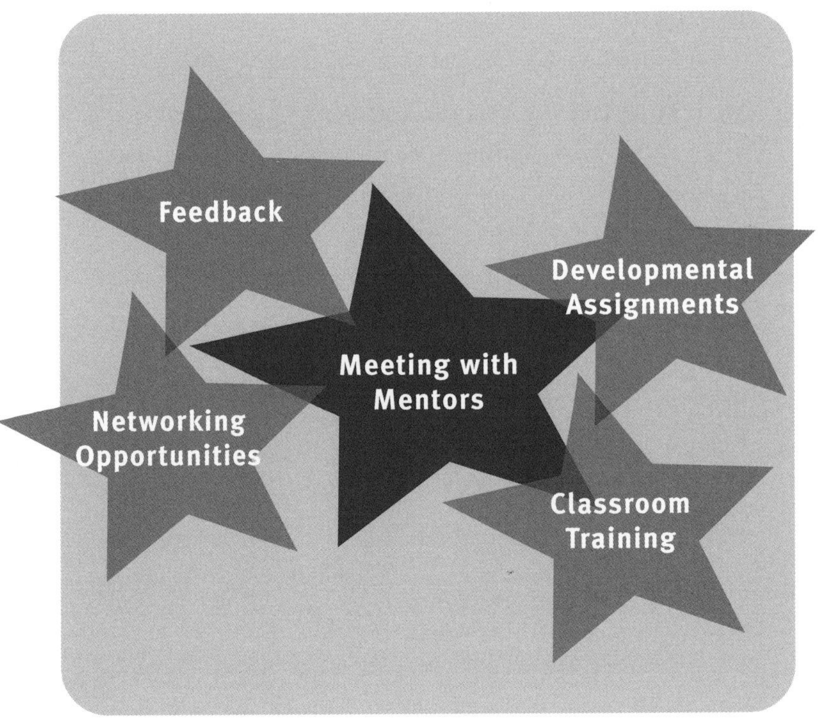

FIVE POPULAR TYPES OF INDIVIDUAL LEARNING EXPERIENCES

1. Meeting with Mentors

The most important feature of a formal mentoring program is, of course, its meetings with mentors. Mentorees will have the opportunity to capitalize on the wisdom of a mentor's experience. This relationship will be based on a careful assessment of the mentoree's developmental needs.

2. Feedback

Confidential self-assessment and multi-rater feedback are two vehicles that can help mentorees target developmental needs and develop effective learning plans. Two popular examples:

- **DISC Self Feedback** (Also known as **Managing for Success®**). **DISC** is a behavioral assessment tool that provides participants an opportunity to immediately increase their knowledge of self and others. **DISC** clarifies individual work styles, how styles effect job performance, and how the mentor and mentoree can work together to build on strengths and overcome weaknesses.

- **Multi-Rater Feedback** – Another popular tool is multi-rater feedback (also known 360 degree feedback). The multi-rater feedback process gives participants a comprehensive perspective of how their actions are being perceived by others. The mentoree rates himself, and enlists others — his immediate supervisor, peers, direct reports, customers — to rate him as well. This valuable information, gathered from a wide range of perspectives, can help the mentoree eliminate blind spots and may also shed light on strengths and areas needing improvement.

360 FEEDBACK

The following excerpt from a mentoree provides insight into the effectiveness and value of 360 feedback:

"I had no idea how my behavior had been impacting my career. This was the first time I have ever gotten honest and candid feedback."

During a 360 degree feedback process, the mentoree's peers and colleagues revealed that although he was technically competent, his behavior was very intimidating and was perceived as unapproachable. This insightful feedback helped the mentoree control his intensity and temper and put more effort in building interpersonal relationships with his co-workers.

3. Networking Opportunities

Employees involved in formal mentoring should always be looking for new opportunities to expand their networks (for example, attending meetings at higher levels than they would normally encounter in their jobs). Participating in a variety of networking opportunities will help mentorees to develop important working relationships, gain exposure to people at different levels and increase visibility. The mentor

NETWORKING OPPORTUNITIES

The following comments on the value that mentoring played in expanding their network were generated from employees involved in a formal mentoring process:

- "One of the strengths of the formal mentoring program was the opportunity for employees to be exposed to others in the organization through the mentor. This gives the employee experience in meeting colleagues from other parts of the organization and lets them gain a broader sense of some of the important issues."

- "A valuable strength of the mentoring program is the nationwide networking opportunities. Participants get the benefits from others who may or may not be involved in their own functional or geographic area."

can serve as an excellent networking resource by introducing the mentoree to key people to whom he or she would not normally have access.

4. Formal Classroom Training

Classroom training can serve as a powerful learning experience as long as it is "timely." Formal training gives employees an opportunity to build conceptual awareness and skills. Mentorees also gain from sharing trade tips and techniques and networking with participants from other public and private organizations. A key outcome of formal training will be the mentoree's ability to apply their new skills on-the-job.

5. Developmental Assignments

A developmental assignment, or "learning by doing," is one of the most effective ways to grow. For many people, this is the best way to develop a new skill or demonstrate a new capability. Whenever possible, successful mentoring programs will encourage employees to use "real work" to learn and practice new skills. Highly effective learning can occur on the job while accomplishing an activity valued by the organization. Some Mentoring Design Teams set a requirement that each mentoree incorporate a developmental assignment into their learning plan for the program. Again, the Mentoring Design Team's choice should be driven by the overall goals of the program.

DEVELOPMENTAL ASSIGNMENTS

The US Customs Service understands the value of ambitious developmental assignments and have incorporated week-long shadowing assignments into their mentoring program. These shadowing assignments provide field employees the opportunity to observe first-hand the day to day activities of Customs Headquarters which include budget, personnel and equal opportunity. A special feature of the shadowing experience is a relevant writing assignment that addresses a current business need (e.g., responding to a request for information from the Washington, DC corporate office). Employees also prepare reports on insights gained during the shadowing assignment and any lessons learned. (USCS, SAIC New Orleans, 1999).

SPECIFIC EXAMPLES OF DEVELOPMENTAL ASSIGNMENTS

Effective developmental assignments meet the following criteria:

- They address an area that is important to the learner.
- They are manageable in scope.
- They produce a concrete result.
- They give employees a chance to prove themselves.
- They are likely to succeed.

Below are specific examples of developmental assignments that enhance employee development:

Shadowing Experience – Some of the most dramatic learning can result from observing key individuals in action. The opportunity to learn from watching another's performance will help mentorees develop greater skill, knowledge and organizational insight.

Team Project or Task Force – Mentorees often learn a great deal by participating on a task force or special team project outside their own technical or functional specialty. This type of project provides mentorees with an opportunity to work with or manage new groups of people, address "real time" problems collectively as a team, overcome unexpected challenges and learn from others under difficult circumstances.

Benchmarking a Model Organization – Benchmarking involves searching for the best possible practices that will help the organization, as a whole, improve performance. The first step involves identifying an area that needs improvement and then finding specific organizations with a reputation for excellence in that area. The mentorees then study those organizations' methods and approaches and implement (or recommend the implementation of) the practices that will improve their own organization's performance.

Leading a Cross-Functional Team – To increase their expertise and leadership skills, some mentorees volunteer to lead or participate in a cross-functional team that brings together a wide variety of backgrounds, experiences and personalities.

THINGS TO KEEP IN MIND WHEN PLANNING THE PROGRAM PURPOSE AND DESIGN:

- Make individual learning relevant to organizational goals.
- Build visible, top management support.
- Target key skills for development.
- Create a comprehensive and connected process.
- Prepare the people involved.
- Evaluate and fine-tune often.

PRACTICAL EXAMPLES AND TECHNIQUES

Establish Relevance

It is important to establish early on that the program is relevant to the needs of the organization and its people. Some program designers have found it helpful to establish program relevance even before recruiting a Mentoring Design Team. This can be accomplished through a series of needs assessments and focus groups.

Questions to Consider:

- Why establish a formalized mentoring program?
- What is the organization's philosophy of mentoring?
- What key organizational priorities or issues can a formalized mentoring program address or support?
- How, specifically, will the organization benefit from a formal mentoring program?
- Is the program linked to another program: diversity, career/leadership development, new employee orientation, recruitment and retention?
- Is the organization willing to invest time and money in this program?
- If not, what steps could be taken to raise the organization's willingness to invest time and money in this program?

PRACTICAL EXAMPLES AND TECHNIQUES

Create Program Purpose, Goals and Objectives

One of the first major responsibilities of the Mentoring Design Team is to create a compelling program purpose. With a compelling purpose, the program will have a direction that will guide the formulation of the program goals and objectives.

Questions to Consider:

Imagine five years from today, when the mentoring program is operating at its best:

- What will the people be saying about the results of the program?
- How will participants be describing their experience in the program?
- Most importantly, what are the skills and competencies targeted for development?

PRACTICAL EXAMPLES AND TECHNIQUES

Define Group and Individual Learning Experiences

Mentoring programs are most effective when participants clearly understand what is expected of them. When designing the program features, be sure to clarify both the group and individual learning experiences. Also remember to keep the program relevant to its participants as well as to the organization as a whole.

Questions to Consider:

- What are the recommended group learning experiences?
- Are any of the group learning experiences mandatory?
- What are the recommended individual learning experiences?

NOTES

NOTES

5

Identify Mentors and Mentorees

STEP 2

THE ROLE OF MENTOR AND MENTOREE will be a new experience for many people. It is important for the Mentoring Design Team to give careful thought to the kinds of people who will succeed in and contribute to the mentoring program. Step 2 gives the Mentoring Design Team an opportunity to:

- Identify the selection criteria for mentors and mentorees.
- Design the selection process.
- Clarify what is expected of participants, both in terms of their roles and time commitments.
- Design a marketing and communication plan.

Identify the Selection Criteria

The selection criteria for mentors and mentorees will be based on the stated goals of the program. For example, if the goal of the mentoring program is to develop a future pool of leaders, then the program will look for applicants (mentorees) who have leadership potential and mentors who are themselves leaders. Alternately, if the program is oriented toward career development, then the application process will target self-motivated learners (mentorees) as well as mentors who have a good track record of advancing their own careers.

DESIGN THE SELECTION PROCESS

There are a variety of approaches that can be used to identify and select participants. Three of the most popular approaches are:

1. Voluntary or self-nomination.
2. A personal recommendation by a supervisor, peer or colleague.
3. Nomination by the Mentoring Design Team (for mentor selections only).

DESIGN THE SELECTION PROCESS

A Directorate within the Department of Defense successfully implemented the third approach for recruiting mentors for their mentoring program. The Mentoring Design Team wanted to make it an "honor" to be nominated as a mentor and created a list of desirable mentors. The Program Champion personally hand-carried over fifty invitations to the pre-nominated mentors. The response rate was overwhelmingly positive and the mentors lived up to their reputations.

The most important criterion for selection as a mentor or mentoree is the participant's level of commitment. The program's coordinators will look for applicants who show a commitment to mentoring for the greater good of the organization. The recruitment process should attract individuals who are interested in building a high performing workplace and who are also interested in challenging themselves personally and professionally.

BEGIN EDUCATING PARTICIPANTS THE MOMENT THEY APPLY

It is essential to start educating participants about mentoring from the moment they apply. Consider framing the application form in a way that challenges the applicant to self-reflect:

- Do I realistically have the time to commit?
- What do I have to offer?
- What am I looking for in a mentor/mentoree?
- Will my supervisor approve?
- How will mentoring help me?

At the same time, ensure that the application forms are easy to complete and collect only the necessary information. Lengthy application forms are too cumbersome to complete and to read. Keep the process short and efficient, for everyone's benefit. Whenever possible, consider web-based tools. (See Appendix A for details).

CLARIFY WHAT IS EXPECTED OF THE PARTICIPANTS

Mentors and mentorees bring different needs and expectations to a mentoring program and partnership. Roles, responsibilities and time commitments need to be clearly defined early in the program. Having clear expectations from the start enables the Mentoring Design Team to market the program to the right people and to target participants who will succeed in and benefit from a formal mentoring process.

The Mentor's Role

For centuries, mentors have offered valuable advancement strategies and protection at critical points in a person's career. But that traditional mentoring approach has changed. Today's mentors *support* rather than direct and *stretch* rather than protect. Rather than smooth the way to advancement, today's dynamic mentors help employees position themselves with the skills, knowledge and people needed to advance their own careers.

Four Main Mentor Roles

The most effective mentors tend to play four main roles: Teacher, Guide, Counselor and Challenger (Drahosz & Rhodes, 1997).

Teacher

In the Teacher role, a mentor helps the mentoree to assess his career goals and outline plans to achieve them. In this role, the mentor takes time to understand where the mentoree is coming from, what he values and what he hopes to become. As Teacher, the mentor will suggest developmental opportunities that give the mentoree a chance to stretch outside of his comfort zone, leverage his skills, and build confidences in his unique abilities. Here's how past mentorees have described their mentor in the Teacher role:

MENTORS IN THE TEACHER ROLE

"He had very candid career discussions with me."

"She helped identify developmental activities appropriate for my career goals."

"He kept in touch with the progress I was making toward my development goals."

Guide

As Guide, the mentor helps the mentoree navigate the political workings of the organization. In the Guide role, a mentor shares the "big picture" (i.e. where the organization is going and why the mentoree's work is important). The mentor will also get actively involved in expanding the mentoree's network and challenge her to develop relationships with key players at higher levels. Here are some comments from mentorees describing how their mentor performed the Guide role:

MENTORS IN THE GUIDE ROLE

"He helped me gain a non-technical perspective of the organization."

"My mentor introduced me to several key people in her network."

"She helped me understand the mission of our program area and why our work mattered."

Counselor

The mentor as Counselor fosters learning through self-discovery by encouraging the mentoree to think for himself and to draw his own conclusions. A mentor is not a problem solver; she is most helpful when she teaches a mentoree how to trust his own abilities and tap into his own inner wisdom. The adage "Give a man a fish and you feed him for a day; teach a man to fish and you feed him for a lifetime" describes the goal of the mentor as Counselor. Here are some mentorees' comments about their mentor in the Counselor role:

MENTORS IN THE COUNSELOR ROLE

"My mentor was good at encouraging, but not forcing his ideas."

"Great sounding board, non-judgmental."

"Listened with his heart and his head."

Challenger

The mentor as Challenger helps the mentoree uncover blind spots in her behavior and performance. In this role, the mentor provides developmental feedback on her strengths as well as her weaknesses. In essence, the mentor in the Challenger role will, metaphorically, hold up a mirror and allow the mentoree to see how her actions impact others and, ultimately, herself. Here is how mentorees have described their mentor in the Challenger role:

MENTORS IN THE CHALLENGER ROLE

"When giving feedback, she always gave solid reasons and explanations."

"He pointed out strengths I didn't realize I had."

"She made developmental suggestions and allowed me to move at my own pace."

In large measure, the success of a mentoring partnership will depend on how well the program has identified and clarified mentor roles and expectations. To ensure productive partnerships, it is critical that the mentor commits to making mentoring a priority, and to stretching him or herself to take on all four of these critical roles.

THE MENTOREE'S ROLE

The Mentoring Design Team needs to define its expectations not only of its mentors, but also of its mentorees. Successful mentorees share three core characteristics: a desire to learn, a commitment to being mentored and the initiative to follow-through and take charge of their own careers. Mentorees involved in a formal mentoring program usually discover that they benefit from mentoring to the degree to which they apply themselves. There are four key roles of a successful mentoree: Learner, Planner, Communicator and Driver (Drahosz & Rhodes, 1997). Each role is explained in greater detail below:

Learner

In the role of Learner, the mentoree continuously looks for opportunities to grow and develop. This often involves asking for feedback, reflecting on experiences (both successes and setbacks) and developing new skills and abilities. Here's how past mentors have described their mentoree in the Learner role:

MENTOREES IN THE LEARNER ROLE

"Continually strived for improvement."

"Used the results of our sessions to improve his effectiveness in the organization."

"Looked for ways to improve in her current position while seeking other opportunities that were on the path to reach her goal."

Planner

As Planner, the mentoree maintains a clear sense of where he is going and tracks and evaluates progress along the way. He comes to mentoring meetings prepared with a concise outline of mentoring topics and issues to be discussed with his mentor. Here are some comments from mentors describing how their mentoree executed the Planner role:

MENTOREES IN THE PLANNER ROLE

"Explored how she wanted her career to progress. "

"Took responsibility to schedule meetings."

"He gave priority to the mentoring relationship; he attended the meetings we scheduled and was fully engaged in the process."

Communicator

As Communicator, the mentoree openly discusses goals, challenges and concerns with the mentor. In addition, she keeps the supervisor informed of her progress in the mentoring program. Here are some mentors comments about their mentoree in the Communicator role:

MENTOREES IN THE COMMUNICATOR ROLE

"He really opened up to me. "

"She gave me good feedback on what worked and what didn't work."

"Communication was great. Even if we could not meet, we checked in with one another. My mentoree was very willing to grow and made it a pleasure to spend time with him."

Driver

In the Driver role, the mentoree maintains momentum in the learning process by initiating and following through on mentoring meetings and commitments. Here is how mentors have described their mentoree in the Driver role:

MENTOREES IN THE DRIVER ROLE

"She took ownership of the process. I helped my mentoree, but she did not use me as a crutch."

"She was very engaged during our meetings and worked off the items on her mentoring plan quickly."

"He brought enthusiasm to his work, the relationship, as well as optimism and excitement about the future. "

THE PIVOTAL ROLE OF THE MENTOREE'S SUPERVISOR

The lack of support from a supervisor can be a major obstacle for a mentoree. Without strong supervisory support and "buy-in" at the beginning of the program, a mentoree may feel uncomfortable investing time and energy to the relationship. Mentoring really takes hold in an organization when the mentorees' supervisors see their employees grow on the job. This is the ultimate test for whether or not mentoring is relevant to the needs of the organization. It is important to explore ways to involve supervisors in the developmental process. This is not always easy, since supervisors may want to support, but not interfere, in the mentoring relationship. Here are a few ways to gain the supervisor's support:

- **Negotiate Clear Agreements.** The mentoree may feel more comfortable spending time in mentoring activities if he or she has negotiated clear agreements with the supervisor in advance. The supervisor can then lend more authentic support by helping the mentoree remove any roadblocks to active participation in the program. This might include prioritizing work assignments to accommodate long-term training events as well as weekly mentoring meetings.

- **Seek Input.** In many cases, a supervisor is able to provide a more comprehensive view of the mentoree's developmental needs. Additionally, the supervisor might be able to help the mentoree find developmental opportunities in everyday work experiences or assignments. Mentors must be extremely careful not to overstep their boundaries in the employee/supervisor relationship. It is suggested that mentors meet or speak with the supervisor only in the presence of their mentoree.

- **Seek Developmental Feedback.** The supervisor can be an excellent source of developmental feedback. They can reinforce the learning that is occurring by providing timely feedback and opportunities to practice new skills.

- **Keep Communication Lines Open.** Keeping the supervisor informed of progress in the mentoring program is an excellent way for the mentoree to foster the supervisor's ongoing support. The more progress the supervisors see, the more likely they are to continue supporting the mentoring program and associated activities.

CLARIFY TIME COMMITMENTS

The mentoring program design should give participants a clear idea of the time commitment involved in the mentoring program. Most successful programs encourage mentoring partners to commit to a 12-month formal mentoring relationship. At the end of the year, the formal mentoring support will end and participants will be invited to continue their partnership informally, as well as to attend any future mentoring forums and workshops.

The mentoring partners should be willing to meet at least one hour per week with the understanding that the time demands may taper off as the relationship matures. The mentoree and mentor will usually work together to determine how the scheduling best meets their individual needs. Generally, those partnerships who commit less time find that they are less than satisfied with the outcome and that too little contact hinders the effectiveness of the mentoring process.

THE MENTOREE'S TIME COMMITMENT

It is important that the mentorees know that they are dedicating themselves to a year of career growth and developmental opportunities. The investment of time from the

MENTOREE TIME COMMITMENT

Many mentorees worry about whether or not they can devote the necessary time to mentoring. The vast majority of our research indicates that this concern is seldom borne out in experience. According to participants in several formally sponsored mentoring programs, 80% of the partnerships met four hours a month, which indicates that most people were able to find the time to devote to the mentoring process and most were motivated enough to do so. In addition, 87% of the mentorees' supervisors who responded to the same survey agreed that the overall benefits of the program were worth the time commitment required of mentorees.

mentorees is significant because of the additional time they will dedicate to developmental activities (networking activities, formal training, shadowing assignments, etc.).

THE MENTOR'S TIME COMMITMENT

For mentors, finding extra time in addition to an already-busy schedule can be a challenge. Yet successful mentors are those who care enough about the mentoring process to make it a priority. Many find their commitment to the mentoring process increases with experience, for it brings them enormous personal and professional rewards. This is one of the many rewarding outcomes for mentors—they receive at least as much from the process as they give.

DESIGN A MARKETING PLAN

A well thought-out marketing plan is a useful tool for the Mentoring Program Coordinator and Design Team to use in the advertisement and selling of the program. A clear strategy will help highlight the multi-dimensional features of formal mentoring. Volunteer mentors and mentorees will need to become aware of the opportunities that are available to them, feel like the mentoring experience will benefit them and understand how to apply to the program.

MARKETING STRATEGIES

The Program Coordinator and Program Champion should maintain a visible presence throughout the marketing and mentoring process. Formal mentoring events such as the mentoring orientation and developmental training, mentoring forums, and program graduation are great vehicles for communicating the features and benefits of the Mentoring Program and its impact on the organization as well as mentors and mentorees.

There are two approaches to marketing the mentoring program: an active approach which is more hands-on and a passive approach, which is more reserved and subtle. Both approaches are important as people process information differently. What works for one person may or may not work for others.

A Hands On Approach

Networking. Contact friends, colleagues and organizational leaders. Ask if they would be interested in signing up to the program. Get additional names to contact, especially potential mentors. *Note: Personal invitations and word of mouth are the best advertisements for a mentoring program in its beginning stage.*

Informational Briefings. Volunteer to speak at a staff meeting, career advisory network or town hall. Encourage people who are leaders in the organization to speak at the briefing. Keep in mind the goal of the informational briefing is to get the word out, educate mentors, mentorees and supervisors of the goals of the mentoring program and to receive possible referrals.

Invitation to Key Personnel. Send a personal note or cover letter with brochures to key people asking them to participate in the program. Be sure to communicate the value they bring to the program and/or the benefits they will gain from participating in the program.

Speaking Engagements. Volunteer to "present" at an upcoming conference, training course or panel. Provide a sneak preview of the benefits of mentoring. Be sure to bring copies of brochures and circulate a sign-in sheet so that follow up information can be sent electronically.

A Subtle Approach

Website. Create a website with a link to the on-line mentoring registration procedures. (See Appendix A for details.) Consider posting a PowerPoint presentation explaining the program goals, features and benefits.

Broadcast E-mail. Write short, snappy tutorials about mentoring. Topics can include what to look for in a mentor or mentoree, professional benefits, success stories, etc.

Mass Mailing (paper, electronic or both). Compile a list of potential candidates who may be interested in the program. Mail them a brochure. To increase the success rate, identify the key personnel in each organization that have the power to influence the participation of potential mentors and mentorees.

Articles. Write articles for the in-house newsletter/bulletin. Educate readers about the program and its features and benefits. Include application forms as well as success anecdotes and testimonies from past mentoring partnerships.

Posters. Place posters announcing the program at strategic points throughout the organization (Cafeteria, bulletin boards, by the elevators, etc.)

THINGS TO KEEP IN MIND WHEN DESIGNING THE SELECTION, APPLICATION AND MARKETING PLAN:

- Begin educating mentors and mentorees the moment they apply.
- Highlight the voluntary and self-directed aspects of the program.
- Assess potential applicants for commitment.
- Allow applicants the opportunity to realistically evaluate whether or not they have the time to dedicate to the process.
- Look for ways to get supervisor support (for example: require signature on the application or recommendation).
- Make it easy to apply. If possible, design an application process that is on-line and web-based.
- Develop a marketing plan that uses a variety of communication vehicles. Include both an active and a subtle approach to getting the word out.

PRACTICAL EXAMPLES AND TECHNIQUES

Designing the Application Process

Design an application process that includes eligibility requirements for participants. Although the most important criteria for selection will be the participant's level of commitment, other aspects to consider include grade levels, job series, types of employment and permanent or part-time status.

In addition to these considerations, there are certain characteristics that a mentor and mentoree should possess to ensure success of the program.

Qualities of the Ideal Mentoree

The ideal mentorees will possess a strong desire to expand their organizational knowledge and skills and be willing to invest time and energy in the mentoring process. They will be proactive in their own career development and exhibit the following characteristics:

- A passion for learning.
- A desire to live up to their own potential.
- Good communication skills.
- Ability to follow through on commitments.
- Receptive to feedback.
- Trustworthiness, ability to keep confidences.

PRACTICAL EXAMPLES AND TECHNIQUES

Qualities of the Ideal Mentor

Mentors will have demonstrated excellence in their careers, possess a positive outlook, and exhibit good communication skills. Most importantly, the ideal mentors will have the time and a strong desire to help others grow personally and professionally. Selection criteria of mentors should possess the following:

- Display highly regarded technical expertise, superb interpersonal skills, and political savvy.
- Willingness to commit time and energy to the mentoring process.
- Willingness to share organizational knowledge, provide objective feedback, and help set developmental goals.
- Capability of working in teams and with diverse groups.
- Willingness to act as a sounding board and confidant.
- Knowledge of the vision, mission, and organizational relationships.
- Openness to feedback and suggestions for improving his/her effectiveness as a mentor.
- Ability to model the characteristics, behaviors, and ethics valued by the organization.
- Willingness to assume responsibility and accountability as a successful mentor.

PRACTICAL EXAMPLES AND TECHNIQUES

Questions to Consider:

- How will potential candidates be educated about the mentoring program?
  - Time commitment?
  - Qualities of a mentor?
  - Qualities of a mentoree?
  - Gaining the supervisor's support?
- Based on the goals of the mentoring program, what criteria will be used to select mentors and mentorees?
- How will the selection criteria be communicated?
- Who will notify those who are not selected and how will they be notified?

PRACTICAL EXAMPLES AND TECHNIQUES

Designing the Marketing Plan

Develop a marketing plan that communicates the features and benefits of the program and solicits participation. Consider several vehicles including word of mouth, brochures, broadcast e-mails, internal newsletters/bulletins, personal invitations, town halls, and staff meetings.

Questions to Consider:

- How will the Mentoring Design Team sell the features of the program?
- Who will endorse the program?
- How will they endorse the program?
- Who will develop and distribute the print and electronic materials?

____

____

____

____

____

NOTES

6

Facilitate a Joint Orientation

STEP 3

AFTER THE PARTICIPANTS have been selected (but before they have been matched into pairs), hold a session for mentors, mentorees and mentorees' supervisors to orient everyone to the formal mentoring program. Educate all three groups on the concept and processes of the mentoring program.

Involvement of the mentorees' supervisors in the first phase of the orientation session is vital. For many supervisors, it can be quite threatening when their employees go to someone else for support and developmental advice. Therefore, educating and familiarizing the supervisors with the mentoring program can ease their concerns and enlist their support.

CLARIFY ROLES AND RESPONSIBILITIES

A key objective of the orientation session is to clarify the participants' roles and responsibilities. While people may initially be excited about the prospect of becoming a mentor or mentoree, they may be daunted by the requirements of a formal program. Having very specific guidelines about time and task requirements in the mentoring program gives participants the information they need to consciously "opt in" to the program, or "opt out" if the commitment seems too overwhelming.

REVIEW THE MATCHING PROCESS

The orientation also serves as a forum for mentors and mentorees to meet each other, receive biographical information about each other and receive instructions for how to submit their mentoring preferences. Giving participants a "voice" in the matching process will foster active participation in the mentoring partnerships. Sometimes a set of matching guidelines is useful to participants for it serves as a tool to assist them in analyzing their needs and expressing their preferences.

For mentorees, the guidelines will include the following:

1. Establish Mentoring Goals.

- Where are you going to be five years from today?
- What are your career aspirations?
- What are you interested in learning to help you get there?
- Do you need to sharpen your technical skills?
    - People skills?
    - Political skills?

2. Describe the Ideal Mentor.

- How would you describe your ideal mentor?

- What capabilities and characteristics would they possess?
- Are you looking for someone with your same functional background or would you like someone to help you bridge into a new career field?
- Are you interested in a mentor who has a certain niche or someone who brings a broad background rich with organizational experience?
- Are you interested in someone who has a similar behavioral style or would you prefer someone who brings a contrasting style?

3. Create a List of Potential Mentors. Once you have clarified your developmental goals and identified your characteristics of an ideal mentor, it is time to create a list of potential candidates. Look for people who possess the traits you wish to develop. Among the mentors selected for this program, prioritize your choices.

For mentors, the guidelines may look something like this:

1. Clarify Mentoring Goals. As a mentor, what kinds of wisdom do you want to pass along? Highlight any or all that apply:

- Leadership/supervisory experience.
- Political, organizational savvy.
- Writing skills.

- Networker.
- Team builder, player.
- Interpersonal skills.
- Communication skills.
- Public speaking skills.
- A successful career path.
- Technical skills.

2. Characterize your Attributes.

- Optimistic, positive attitude.
- Confidant/sounding board.
- Good at challenging people.
- Supportive, safe style.
- Sense of humor.
- Committed to helping people grow and develop.
- Practical and logical.
- Compassionate.

3. Describe the Ideal Mentoree. Once you have clarified your mentoring goals and have identified the characteristics you offer, the next step is to explore the traits to look for in an ideal mentoree.

- How would you describe their qualities, capabilities and character?
- Are you looking for someone who wants to sharpen their technical expertise in a certain business area or

would you prefer someone who wants to broaden their leadership and organizational experience?

- Are you looking for someone who is new to the organization or would you prefer a seasoned employee who has hit a plateau?
- Are you looking for someone who has a similar behavioral style or would you prefer someone who brings a contrasting style to the partnership?

4. List your Preferences. Based on your answers to Questions 1, 2 and 3, prioritize your top five choices for a mentoree.

It is important to stress that individual preferences will be considered, but not guaranteed. The Program Coordinator and Mentoring Design Team will gather all the information and make the appropriate matches based on the mentor's capability to support the mentoree's needs. The key factor to consider when matching is the relevance of the mentor's experience to the career goals of the mentoree.

PRACTICAL EXAMPLES AND TECHNIQUES

Sample Outline of Joint Orientation Session

A typical orientation session consists of the following components:

- Kick-off by the Program Champion.
- Explanation of what mentoring is and why it is important.
- Features of a formal mentoring program (components and milestones).
- Roles and requirements of the participants and mentorees' supervisors.
- What to look for in mentor or mentoree.
- The process for submitting preferences for ideal matches and guidance for making appropriate matches.
- Various activities that enable the participants to get to know each other.

Sample Mentoring Matching Form

Mentor/Mentoree Matching Form

Name:	Jan Doe
Organization:	TTC
Title/Series/Grade:	Vice President
Phone Number:	703-555-1212

---

1) Describe your Ideal Mentor/Mentoree: (Please be very specific)

My ideal mentor is someone who has a strong background in business and people development. He/she should be a senior executive with a solid background.

2) Please list your suggestions for a Mentor/Mentoree in descending order. Provide an explanation as necessary in the text area below:

Rank	Mentor	Explanation
1	Dina	Great interpersonal skills and political savvy.
2	Brian	Strong relationship skills with a solid background in business development.
3	Choose ▼	

3) Please list what you would consider as inappropriate choices for a Mentor in descending order.

Rank	Mentor	Explanation
1	Jen Harris	She is my first line supervisor.

4) I understand that this is an initial screening process and that my choices will be strongly considered but cannot be guaranteed.

NOTES

NOTES

7

Match the Mentoring Partners

STEP 4

WHEN CREATING A FORMAL SYSTEM FOR MATCHING, be sure to give both partners a "voice" in the process. In other words, offer mentors and mentorees an opportunity to screen and select potential partners. Encourage them to use objective criteria based on career and developmental goals. There are a variety of ways to match mentors with mentorees, ranging from formal matches by the Mentoring Design Team to a more informal process, where a mentoree is expected to identify his or her own mentor.

DETERMINE MATCH CRITERIA

Participants often make the mistake of assuming the best mentoring match is someone of similar style. While mentor-mentoree similarity may offer a comfortable relationship, it is not always optimal for the mentoree's learning. The best matches are often the ones that feature differences in experience, behavioral style, location, gender, and race.

Our research has uncovered two key factors that contribute to the success of a mentoring partnership: 1) differences in behavioral style and 2) differences in experience (Drahosz, 1999). Mentors and mentorees will reap the greatest benefits if they can enter the relationship understanding how to identify, respect, and leverage the differences they bring to the mentoring relationship.

A popular tool to identify differences (as well as commonalities) is the DISC style analysis (also known as Managing for Success®). DISC measures the level of intensity a person brings to four areas of behavior (**D**ominance, **I**nfluence, **S**teadiness, **C**ompliance).

DISC

D: How one approaches problems and challenges.
I: How one interacts and influences people.
S: How one responds to change and levels of activity.
C: How one responds to rules and regulations.

The D factor, for example, does not measure whether or not a person can solve problems, but rather measures *how* the person goes about solving problems. The position of each DISC factor provides useful behavioral information and gives mentors a more accurate foundation for suggesting developmental assignments and training opportunities.

With this in mind, the Mentoring Design Team may want to consider using a self-assessment tool as a key program feature in the matching process. (See Appendix C for additional details.)

THE GEOGRAPHIC SEPARATION FACTOR

It is important to understand the implications of pairing a mentoree with a mentor who is located in a different geographical location. The difficulty geographically dispersed partners encounter is the ability to establish and maintain a strong sense of connection. Without the benefit of frequent personal contact, partners find that it takes a bit more effort to keep the personal connection going and growing. Despite these challenges, however, there are also great payoffs. Mentorees can benefit tremendously from the exposure to new people, processes and perspectives that someone in a different location can provide.

While long-distance mentoring can be challenging, it does not need to be a major barrier. There are steps that the mentor or the mentoree can take to strengthen their long-distance relationship:

- Coordinate travel schedules for participants to meet in person whenever possible. If the partners are going to be in the same city on business, consider adding an extra day to the itinerary to spend together.

- Utilize technology, such as videoconferencing and e-mail.
- Keep regularly scheduled phone appointments.
- Prepare for phone conversations. Generate an agenda for the conversation and e-mail items to each other in advance.
- Build in frequent reviews. Periodically assess how the mentoring conversations are working and what might make them work better.

FORMAL MATCHING PROCESS

An example of a formal matching process used by several public and private organizations:

The Mentoring Connection's© (TMC) web-based system recruits volunteers as mentors and identifies mentoree candidates. Biographies are electronically distributed to each group (i.e., mentorees review mentor biographies and mentors review mentoree biographies). Each participant then prioritizes his/her mentor selections in terms of their preferred pairings and identifies any individuals that would be poor or unworkable matches for themselves.

FORMAL MATCHING PROCESS (CONTINUED)

The Program Coordinator and Mentoring Design Team gathers all the information and makes appropriate matches based on the mentor's capability to support the mentoree's needs, as well as the participants' own stated preferences. Matches are based on the following criteria:

1) The mentor and mentoree are not in the same chain-of-command (line of authority) structure.
2) The mentor brings a different knowledge base and experience that is relevant to the mentoree's career goals.
3) The mentor is evaluated as the best to support the mentoree's developmental process.

If at any point the mentor or the mentoree feel the match is inappropriate or not working, they are encouraged to notify the Program Coordinator for coaching assistance or a possible rematch. The program also incorporates a no-fault option for ending a non-productive relationship. (See Chapter 8 for additional information on no-fault terminations.)

THINGS TO KEEP IN MIND WHEN DESIGNING A FORMAL MATCHING PROCESS:

- Link matching criteria to the goals of the program.
- Give mentors and mentorees a voice in the process.
- Build the geographic distance factor into the matching design.
- Encourage diversity in experience, behavior, location, age, gender, and/or race.
- Honor a no-fault option for ending a non-productive partnership.
- Make it easy to preview biographies of potential mentors and mentorees (preferably on-line and web-based).

PRACTICAL EXAMPLES AND TECHNIQUES

Matching Mentorees with Mentors

Every effort should be made to match mentorees with mentors who can best support their development needs. Suggested criteria might include:

- Career fields, work history.
- Location.
- Supervisory/leadership experience.
- Technical expertise.
- Organizational savvy.
- Interpersonal skills.
- DISC behavioral styles.

Questions to Consider:

- How will mentors and mentorees have a "voice" in the matching?
- What are the guidelines for matching?
- What happens if a partnership is not working?
- What are the guidelines for re-matching?

____

____

____

8

Provide Mentoring Training and Tools

STEP 5

TRAINING BOTH MENTORS AND MENTOREES for their roles in the mentoring process is vital to the success of the program, as these roles will be very new to most people. Organizational life teaches us how to manage and be managed, but not necessarily how to learn effectively or to foster someone else's learning.

PREPARING THE PEOPLE INVOLVED

In his research on *Why Mentoring Programs and Relationships Fail,* David Clutterbuck found that "without any training at all, less than one in three pairings will deliver significant results. Training mentors alone raises the success rate to around 65%. Training both and educating line managers about the program pushed the success rate above 90%, with both parties reporting substantial gains." (Clutterbuck, 2002).

The most successful mentoring programs invest time and resources into preparing mentors, mentorees and supervisors for their role. Below is a sample outline for two main structured training events: the "Dynamic Mentoring Workshop" (at the program's official beginning) and the "Mentor the Mentor Series" (throughout the year-long program).

DYNAMIC MENTORING WORKSHOP

The Dynamic Mentoring workshop begins the formal mentoring program with a two-day, structured training experience that is intended to set the partners up for success. This foundational training enables both mentors and mentorees to assume their roles effectively and arranges for the partnerships to work smoothly and confidently throughout the program.

An overview of the training content is as follows:

Preparing the Mentorees

During the workshop, the mentorees (working separately from the mentors) learn how to engage in a successful mentoring partnership and begin to take charge of their careers. Through a series of individual and group activities, mentorees define their learning goals for the program, and are then rejoined by their mentors and continue their planning process in dialogue. Mentors can add great value to the planning process. They are usually at a higher organizational level than the mentoree and often have a better grasp of what skills are necessary and what developmental activities are available. They can also share lessons from past experience. This "action planning process" has three distinct phases: defining career goals, assessing current skill levels, and designing activities to bridge the gap (Drahosz and Rhodes, 1997).

Action Planning Process

- In the first phase of the action planning process, the mentorees identify their career goals and clarify their career expectations.

- During the second phase, mentorees explore their current abilities in relation to their career goals and objectives. Mentorees are encouraged to take a systematic approach in identifying strengths and weaknesses with respect to their career goals. If the Mentoring Design Team has elected to use a multi-rater feedback instrument as part of its design, the results of the feedback instrument can serve as an excellent tool for assessing a person's current performance.

- During the third phase, mentorees identify how to

close the gap between where they are today and where they want to take their careers in the future.

The ultimate product of this process will be a detailed development plan, called the Mentoring Action Plan (MAP). The MAP outlines specific learning activities the mentoree will undertake during the year-long mentoring program. A well-designed plan is what enables mentorees to gain the most benefit from the mentoring partnership and will begin to bridge his or her developmental gaps. The planning process begins at the Dynamic Mentoring Workshop, and usually takes one to two months to complete. This is a process which demands careful thought, dialogue, analysis and planning.

A common mistake people make when designing their MAP is to assume that classroom training is the best and only option for learning. Therefore, the Mentoring Design Team will want to give the mentoring pairs a list of suggested developmental activities (Chapter 4 illustrates possible types of activities) that should be built into their plans. It is the mastery of these developmental milestones that will ensure success in the program.

SAMPLE DEVELOPMENTAL MILESTONES

Each mentoring pair will incorporate the following:

1) one activity that fosters learning by doing (a special assignment),
2) one activity that encourages learning from others (a shadowing experience),
3) one activity that encourages learning from challenging experiences (leading a cross-functional team).

Preparing the Mentors

During the Dynamic Mentoring Workshop, mentors (working separately from the mentorees) will learn how to create a climate where mentorees take responsibility for their own career growth and development. They will also explore, in greater depth, the four mentoring roles — Teacher, Guide, Counselor, and Challenger — and examine the best uses of each role in supporting the mentoree's developmental goals. Mentors will then have a better understanding of their roles and responsibilities and the types of assistance they can provide to the mentoree. They will receive practical, easy-to-use mentoring guides for use during the training program as well as for ongoing career counseling and career planning.

Preparing the Partnerships

An important segment of the Dynamic Mentoring Workshop is to carefully design the individual mentoring partnerships. The pairs will clarify the goals for learning, build structures for meeting and communicating, establish norms for the relationship, and outline their own "style" for working together throughout the year by way of The Mentoring Agreement. The Mentoring Agreement is a key tool for partnership development and will be built on the following:

- **Objectives** of the partnership (identify learning goals).

- **Logistics** of the meetings (when, where, how long).

- **Norms and Ground Rules** for interaction (confidentiality and no-fault termination agreements).

- **Commitment of the Supervisor.** The supervisor plays a key role in the mentoring partnership, and as such, mentoring partnerships should always seek ways to include the supervisor in all phases of the process. For example, they may want to tap the supervisor as a source of feedback and input to the goal-setting process. Or, they may want to ask the supervisor to help identify any on-the-job developmental opportunities that would support the mentoree's learning goals. By including the supervisor from the beginning, the mentoree might feel more supported in their mentoring activities.

  In some extreme cases, the mentoree may choose not to involve their supervisor in his or her mentoring plans. This usually occurs when there is trouble between the supervisor and the employee, or when the employee is ready to change jobs and/or organizations. If this is the case, the mentor and mentoree should discuss this up front, examine the implications for the mentoring process and design appropriate strategies.

- **Confidentiality.** A confidentiality agreement merits careful attention as it is vital for mentoree and mentor to trust each other. Each partner should discuss their concerns about what constitutes a confidentiality agreement and what steps they will take to honor it. One example of a confidentiality agreement might be, "What we discuss stays between the two of us." Another might be, "What we discuss stays between the two of us unless you give me permission to share it with others." The confidentiality agreement covers whatever is necessary for both partners to feel confident that they can share important information without concern for repercussion.

- **Termination.** The mentoring program should offer a no-fault termination to all of its mentoring pairs. If a mentoring relationship has outgrown its usefulness, it is helpful to have a mechanism in place that concludes the relationship without harm to the mentor or the mentoree. Margo Murray (2001) calls this ending a "no-fault conclusion." Murray suggests that this "no-fault" termination feature be a part of the program design and should be emphasized and planned for at the beginning of the mentoring process.

Both the Mentoring Action Plan and Mentoring Agreement may appear at first glance to be quite overwhelming. However, they are an integral part of the mentoring program. Decades of experience in helping organizations implement formal mentoring programs have shown that the truly successful partnerships are the ones that have established a thorough process of planning. The time taken in the pre-planning stage will yield great dividends, as it will free the partners from a great deal of confusion, frustration and miscommunication throughout the year. If mentoring partners are located in different geographic locations, it is recommended that extra care be taken in crafting an agreement that helps the pair compensate for the challenges posed by physical separation and distance.

ONGOING MENTOR TRAINING: THE "MENTOR THE MENTOR" SERIES

Through our experience in managing mentoring programs, we have found it very beneficial to keep mentors actively involved in sharpening their mentoring skills. This concurrent education and learning process benefits:

1) mentorees, who receive increasingly skillful mentoring,
2) mentors, who become better mentors **and** better managers, and
3) the organization, which cultivates a more skilled cadre of leaders.

The "Mentor the Mentor" series consists of five sessions

that deliver both the skills and knowledge that mentors will need at particular points in the life cycle of the mentoring process.

Session I: ***Skills of the Four Mentoring Roles***

This session will help mentors learn how to ask thought-provoking questions and shift their role from wise sage to developmental coach.

Session II: ***Developmental Planning – Setting Learning Goals***

This session helps mentors add value to the developmental planning process and suggests learning experiences based on mentoree needs.

Session III: ***Taking Stock, Gauging Progress and Mid-Course Correction***

The mid-point of a mentoring program is a great place to pause, take stock and gauge mentoring progress. This session gives mentors a chance to reflect on their mentoring journey. They can explore the significance of their mentoring contributions and surface any difficulties that may become larger problems down the road.

Session IV: ***Sustaining Momentum and Renewing Commitment***

This session provides mentors with the opportunity to

renew their commitment as well as sustain momentum in their mentoring partnerships. Participants discuss and explore the challenges that may have arisen within their mentoring partnerships. These may include issues they are working on with their mentoree or questions they have about their own mentoring abilities.

Session V: *Closing the Formal Mentoring Relationship*
This session prepares the mentors for the end of the formal relationship and fosters a sense of appreciative completion. Mentors learn how to help mentorees identify, leverage and celebrate success. Mentors also have the opportunity to explore their role in harvesting learning outcomes and to discuss ideas for continuing to build mentoring as an integral part of the organization's culture.

THINGS TO KEEP IN MIND WHEN DESIGNING THE FORMAL MENTORING TRAINING:

- Clarify confidentiality agreements and expectations early on.
- Build avenues to gain supervisory support.
- Address sensitive issues: how to terminate a partnership, whether or not to involve the supervisor, etc.
- Provide mentors and mentorees with the tools they need to stay on track.

PRACTICAL EXAMPLES AND TECHNIQUES

Develop a Training and Development Plan

Create a training and development plan that prepares mentors, mentorees and supervisors for their role in mentoring.

Questions to Consider:

- What is the timeline?
- Will mentorees complete and follow a Mentoring Agreement and Mentoring Action Plan?
- Will there be a "no-fault" termination option and confidentiality agreement?
- What sort of "make-up" (if any) will be available to participants who miss the training?

NOTES

PRACTICAL EXAMPLES AND TECHNIQUES

Sample Mentoring Action Plan

Vision:

My personal vision is to enable people to be inspired by their own individual talents and to live up to their unlimited potential.

Mentoring Goals and Objectives:

1. To develop a better understanding of the inner workings of the organization.
2. To improve presentation skills.
3. To enhance my reputation as a highly sought-after expert in team building and leadership.

Developmental Opportunity 1: Navigating the Organization

Learning Activity	Competency	Beginning Date	Ending Date	Funding	Status
Interview five key executives regarding how they get things done through informal channels and networks. Note the common themes and discuss with my mentor.	Organizational Knowledge	3/10/2003	3/10/2003	$0.00	Pending
Shadow the Deputy Director for one week. Pay careful attention to how s/he balances the competing demands of multiple stakeholders.	Organizational Knowledge	6/10/2003	6/15/2003	$0.00	Approved

Developmental Opportunity 2: Navigating the Organization

Learning Activity	Competency	Beginning Date	Ending Date	Funding	Status
Develop a presentation on How Leaders Grow Leaders. The presentation will include overheads, handout package and annotated bibliography.	Communication	9/10/2003	11/10/2003	$0.00	Approved
Observe three key executives giving presentation. Note the positive aspects of their presentation styles; note what I'd do differently. Discuss finds with mentor.	Communication	10/10/2003	11/10/2003	$0.00	Approved

PRACTICAL EXAMPLES AND TECHNIQUES

Sample Mentoring Agreement

This agreement will be the foundation of the mentoring partnership. The strength of the agreement will be dependent upon the level of detail in its development. The more detailed the agreement is the more powerful the relationship will be.

Mentoring Objectives: Develop a formal action plan to keep the partnership on track and target. The Mentoring Action Plan will include the following goals and objectives:

1.
2.
3.

Meeting Management: Mentoring meetings will begin and end on time:
When:
Where:
How long:
Frequency of meetings (weekly, bi-weekly, monthly):
What happens if a partner cannot meet?
Who is responsible for rescheduling?

Confidentiality Agreement: The following parameters will be honored:

____

____

(Note: Be sure to clarify assumptions. For example, "What we discuss stays between the two of us.")

No Fault Termination: This is a volunteer partnership. If at any point in the relationship it is not working, the partnership will:

____

____

9

Implementation

STEP 6

ONCE THE MENTORS AND MENTOREES have been selected, matched and trained, the program will move into the implementation phase. Implementation success is often enhanced by a series of structured learning experiences and activities that support the program participants throughout the duration of the program. Without such mechanisms, the partnerships may lose momentum and focus. It is recommended that the Program Coordinator re-energize the mentoring partnerships throughout the year by providing quarterly workshops, mentoring forums, periodic evaluations, and progress reports. Below are some of the activities a Program Coordinator can undertake to support the program during the implementation phase.

PROVIDE CONTINUOUS LEARNING EXPERIENCES

- **Periodic Mentoring Forums.** The Program Coordinator supports the mentoring relationships by coordinating monthly or quarterly learning forums. Not only will the forums provide participants with new information and a forum to exchange ideas and information, but it also gives the Program Coordinator an opportunity to check on the vitality and effectiveness of the relationships.

- **Mid-Point Energizer.** The mid-point of the mentoring program is a great place to evaluate and energize the program participants. Through a series of individual and group activities, the Program Coordinator can assess what areas in both the partnership and the program are working and what areas could benefit from fine-tuning. By bringing lessons learned in the program to a conscious level, participants are better able to understand the significance of their mentoring experiences and make quick adjustments if and when necessary. (Details of the mid-point evaluation are contained in Chapter 10, Evaluating and Tracking Progress.)

- **Training Opportunities, Relevant Articles, and Books.** Keep mentors and mentorees aware of upcoming events and learning vehicles (books, articles, rotational assignments, etc.). Encourage information sharing regarding upcoming activities and training events.

- **End of Program Celebration and Evaluation.** Just as the mentoring partners benefit from a mid-program energizing session, a formal session at the end of the program can be equally enriching. This session gives mentors and mentorees the opportunity to take stock of their growth over the past year and explores the part mentoring played in enhancing their performance.

BUILD ORGANIZATIONAL SUPPORT AT ALL LEVELS

As employees go through the mentoring process, they will be watching for signs that the program is supported by management at all levels. There are many ways in which the Program Coordinator can acquire and build this visible support. For example, they will look for opportunities to publicly recognize and reward employees who are developing themselves and others. They also must be willing to troubleshoot the organizational obstacles that may get in the way of employee development and communicate those obstacles and potential solutions to top management. Lastly and most importantly, the Program Coordinator must create opportunities for senior leaders to play highly visible roles in developmental events. Consider the following to promote high-level support for the mentoring program:

Create Opportunities for Mentor/Mentoree Exposure and Recognition

- Have mentorees make presentations to management that illustrate the positive results of their mentoring activities.

- Show appreciation (in a public forum) for the mentorees' initiative and the mentors' dedication to people development.
- Provide updated progress reports to senior leaders.
- Encourage mentorees to undertake projects that have the potential to benefit other parts of the organization.

Anticipate Barriers

- Schedule mentoring training events outside busy periods.
- Increase the travel portion of the mentoring program budget to allow mentoring partners located in different geographical locations the opportunity to travel to each other's sites.
- Provide developmental ideas to mentorees. Consider establishing a "resource bank" of learning activities for mentoring participants. These activities could be pre-screened by senior management and thus be deemed worthwhile to the organization.
- Ask mentorees' supervisors to exempt them from lengthy travel schedules for the duration of the mentoring program.
- Serve as a main point of contact for trouble-shooting problems and challenges (i.e., problems in the partnership or with supervisors regarding participation in the program).

Enlist Senior Management's Visible Support

- Ask senior leadership to communicate to all managers in the organization what the goals of the mentoring program are and what the expectations are of all managers in supporting the mentoring program.
- Ask upper management to personally "check in" on how the relationships are progressing.
- Coordinate a shadowing assignment or schedule lunch with a senior manager.
- Encourage the Program Champion to play a key role in the events that kick off and wrap up the mentoring program.

HONOR THE INTEGRITY OF THE PROGRAM

A formal mentoring program is a great tool for demonstrating that the organization cares about its employees and is willing to invest time, money and resources in helping employees grow personally and professionally. With this in mind, it is important to deliver on promises made. A mentoring program will quickly lose credibility and momentum if it fails to follow through on those promises at the beginning of the program. Consider the following actions that sustain program integrity:

- **Keep Matching (and Re-Matching) Information Confidential.** The Program Coordinator will want to maintain the confidentiality when matching or re-matching mentoring partners.

- **Follow Through on Advertised Commitments.** Be frugal and honest with program changes, especially when introducing a change that might look to be inconsistent with a prior commitment. Make good on initial promises and notify participants candidly when you cannot.

    For example:
    At the beginning of the program you promised that mentors and mentorees would have at least three face-to-face meetings, but due to budget constraints the program can only bring geographically dispersed partners together one time during the course of the year.

To maintain employee trust and program credibility, deal openly and honestly with changes to program design. Reassure the mentoring partnerships that you care about the unexpected changes and are actively working to correct them.

- **Honor a No-fault Termination.** Make it as comfortable as possible for partners to opt out of the partnership if it is no longer serving them. The Program Coordinator can help the partnerships to dissolve if he or she suspects that the partnership is in trouble and/or not actively participating in the program.

MAINTAIN ACCOUNTABILITY

Most difficulties that arise in a formal mentoring process can be traced back to the way the program was planned, supported and managed. Some Program Coordinators may provide so much structure that they suffocate the creativity of the mentoring relationships, while others may offer too little guidance and program oversight. The Program Coordinator's role is to strike a delicate balance between autonomy and accountability as well as self-direction and responsibility. Here are a few suggestions:

- **Follow Through on Incomplete or Unsubmitted Mentoring Action Plans and Mentoring Agreements.** Most formal mentoring programs will ask participants to submit their Mentoring Action Plans and Mentoring Agreements to the Program Coordinator. The Program Coordinator may want to follow up with anyone not responding to the call. In some cases, the reason the mentoree has not followed through with their plan is because they are in need of developmental coaching. Be willing to provide guidance and assistance to both the mentoree and mentor in developmental planning or make a recommendation that the mentoree seek career counseling assistance.

- **Pay Attention to Attendance at Mentoring Forums and Training Events.** A mentor or mentoree who consistently fails to attend required training or checkpoints may be signaling that their partnership is in trouble. Consider personally following up with the person to find out why he or she is not attending. This information can be an excellent "early warning system" for problems such as workload conflicts, lack of interest or initiative, or a larger issue relating to incompatibility of the mentoring match.

- **Check In On Time Commitments.** The Program Coordinator can reinforce the commitment needed to sustain the mentoring relationship by periodically assessing time commitments. Consider asking the following: How often are you meeting? Are you satisfied with the amount of time you are investing? What changes could be made to increase the amount of time dedicated to the mentoring partnership?

SIGNS OF A PARTNERSHIP IN TROUBLE

All mentoring relationships will go through different phases of development. It is important to help mentors and mentorees learn how to effectively address and/or anticipate potential issues that may arise. More often than not, there are clear indicators when a partnership is not working. You may see either or both parties in the partnership exhibit the following behaviors:

- Lack of participation in structured training.
- Lack of follow-through on commitments (such as submitting the MAP, or meeting with the mentoring partner).
- Lack of visible enthusiasm or energy.
- Complaints about the mentoring partner.
- Either partner reporting feeling "stuck" or frustrated.

As the Program Coordinator, it is appropriate to follow up with either or both parties if you see this kind of behavior and help the partners identify and work through the issue(s) at the core of the problem. Some of these issues may include:

- Conflicting goals or values.
- Violation of a confidentiality agreement.
- Lack of trust.
- Infrequent interaction.
- Stagnant learning/growing.

Many of these issues, when identified early, can be successfully addressed and the relationship can get back on track. Occasionally, as in the violation of confidentiality, the relationship may be damaged to the point that it cannot be saved. This would be an appropriate use of the "no-fault termination" option, and, if the timing permits, you may be able to pair the mentoree up with a new mentor.

ENDING THE FORMAL MENTORING RELATIONSHIP

There are enormous benefits to ending the mentoring relationship in a careful and deliberate fashion. It is often easiest for us to just say "Thanks" and move on, or to avoid the discomfort of closure altogether. Yet the end of the mentoring relationship can be a powerful opportunity for both partners to take stock of their gains and to express their gratitude for each other's contributions. For a majority of partnerships, the mentoring experience proves to be a uniquely rewarding one, so providing a positive sense of closure is an excellent way to honor the partnership.

When it is time for the relationship to end, the mentor and mentoree should close with the following actions:

- Review the original purpose for the relationship and acknowledged goals of the mentoree.
- Compile the accomplishments.
- Strategize the next steps for the mentoree.
- Recognize the successful contributions of the mentoree and mentor.
- Celebrate successes!

TROUBLE-SHOOTING TIPS

The following trouble-shooting section addresses the most frequently asked questions from the mentor, mentoree and Program Coordinator.

Frequently Asked Questions by Mentorees:

Q: I do not want to take advantage of my mentor's good will. How do I make sure that I am not over-stepping my boundaries?

A: The Mentoring Agreement should be used as your guide throughout the partnership. The more detailed the agreement, the clearer the boundaries will be. It is important that you are both "up front" with your needs and expectations. You will also need to be specific about the time that will be invested and respectful of the professional responsibilities of your mentor.

Q: My mentor isn't returning my calls. What should I do?

A: Keep in mind that your mentor has multiple responsibilities and time constraints of his or her own. You may want to try another method of contact such as e-mail. If you do not get a response after three tries, you may want to investigate. Is there a big deadline looming on the horizon? Or is an there a personal conflict (illness, child care issues, etc.)? If you feel that your mentor's interest and time is waning, it never hurts to ask about it.

Q: I feel torn between my mentor's and supervisor's advice and philosophies. Whose advice should I heed?
A: As the adage goes, "Take what you like and leave the rest." As long as it does not jeopardize your current position, take the advice you feel most comfortable with. Use your own judgment. Remember, more often than not, there is more than one way to do something.

Q: I know my mentor means well, but I do not feel that I am getting that much from the partnership.
A: The mentoring relationship is the perfect place to sharpen effective diplomacy skills. It can be a wonderful developmental experience to learn how to ask for what you want and to initiate a "fine tuning" session that will benefit the both of you.

Frequently Asked Questions by Mentors:

Q: My mentoree does not appear to be any closer to his/her goals since the onset of this program. What can I do to "jump start" this partnership?
A: There could be many factors that may be impacting this slow progression toward your mentoree's goals. You may just want to take time out for lunch or coffee and play the "counselor" role for a bit. Is there trouble on a personal level or a conflict in the office? A little listening can go a long way. If there does not appear

to be problems of that sort, then you may want to play the "challenger" role. Tactfully express your concerns to your mentoree about their lack of progress. You may want to provide the mentoree with new challenges that they could use to energize and focus their learning process.

Q: Although I did take the time to fully evaluate the time involved in becoming a mentor, I feel as though my mentoree is asking for more time than I can spare.
A: At your next scheduled meeting, review the Mentoring Agreement that you and your mentoree crafted at the beginning of the program. Ask them about their thoughts on the time that was agreed upon in the Mentoring Agreement. Be candid with your concerns with the extra time being requested and ask your mentoree to recommit to the original agreement.

Q: My mentoree is having problems with her supervisor. What should my level of involvement be?
A: It is best not to take sides. It is more helpful to your mentoree to support her in finding her own solution, rather than actively involving yourself in it. The best way to assist your mentoree in this situation is through the Counselor and Guide roles. Encourage your mentoree to assess the problem herself and develop her own solution.

Frequently Asked Questions by Mentoring Partners:

Q: What if we do not have any "chemistry" with one another? Is our partnership doomed?

A: Some of the best mentoring relationships are those partnerships where there are significant differences between the mentor and mentoree. Although these relationships can be a bit of a challenge at times, these partnerships can be extremely rewarding as long as trust and respect are present on both sides.

Q: Should I be able to trust my mentor or mentoree?

A: Absolutely. Trust is the foundation of the relationship and a crucial element in the success of your mentoring partnership. It is important to take great care when developing your mentoring agreement. Issues of trust and confidentiality are the cornerstone of that agreement and should be discussed openly and candidly from the onset.

Frequently Asked Questions by Program Coordinators:

Q: The mentoree has an unrealistic expectation of receiving a promotion. What should I tell him?

A: The mentoring process (formal or informal) offers no guarantees. Mentoring offers mentorees an opportunity to position themselves with skills, people and an environment for success. They are more marketable as a result of working with a mentor, but the increased marketability does not guarantee a promotion.

Q: The Mentoring Design Team does not seem to be involved in the program. What should I do to get them to share more of the workload?
A: The Mentoring Design Team's role is to help develop the program and provide guidance and oversight, not to implement the program. The Program Coordinator is responsible for the majority of the program management and coordination. If the workload of this role is too great, consider getting an "Assistant Program Coordinator" to assist with the day-to-day activities and events.

Q: The supervisor refuses to let the mentoree participate in mentoring activities. Should I get involved?
A: Yes. As part of the formal mentoring support system, the key role of the Program Coordinator is to facilitate communication between mentorees and supervisors regarding participation in the program.

Q: A mentor broke his confidentiality agreement with his mentoree. What advice should I give the mentoree?
A: When a partnership's confidentiality agreement has been broken it is difficult to rebuild trust in the

relationship. The mentoree will need to decide if it is worth the time and energy required to re-establish trust. Be sure to remind the mentoree that he or she can always close down the formal mentoring partnership through the established "no-fault" termination agreement.

Q: I am not sure if the mentoring partnerships are progressing toward their mentoring goals. What role should I play?
A: Once the mentoring partnerships have been matched and the participants trained, a key role of the Program Coordinator is to provide ongoing support. Let the mentoring participants know that you are available for advice and guidance. Publish success stories in monthly newsletters. Offer tips and strategies such as how to keep mentoring meetings on track, ideas for developmental activities, do's and don'ts for building trust, etc. Facilitate quarterly mentoring forums and brown bag workshops. Look for creative ways to keep the program on the participants' radar screen.

NOTES

10

Evaluate and Track Progress

STEP 7

AN EFFECTIVE EVALUATION SYSTEM relies on the assumption that investing in human resource development is well worth the time, money and resources required. There are two critical checkpoints in this process: six months after the program begins and at its conclusion. Typically, a Program Coordinator monitors the program's effectiveness through:

1) Telephone interviews with participants.
2) Feedback from written mid-point and end of program reviews.
3) Group feedback sessions conducted at the mid-point and at the end of a program.

There are special considerations for evaluating the effectiveness of mentoring relationships in a formal development system. In her work with facilitated mentoring, Margo Murray (2001), cautioned that it is difficult to isolate a single factor when measuring the effectiveness of developmental relationships.

Therefore, to make the evaluation meaningful, Murray (2001) suggests that program evaluators ask two key questions before conducting an evaluation: 1) What do we need to know about the impact of the program on the organization, and 2) How will we use the information once we have collected it?

MID-POINT EVALUATION

The mid-point evaluation is three-fold. First, it serves as a re-energizer for both the program and its participants. Second, it uncovers any elements of the program that are not working and offers corresponding "fine tuning." And third, and most importantly, it should examine the individual partnerships and assess their growth and accomplishments. The following sample evaluation criteria should serve as a guide in the creation of specific evaluation questions:

Evaluation Criteria	What to Ask
Overall program effectiveness The first measure of program success is the degree of benefit experienced by the individuals who participated in it. While it is easy to focus solely on the mentorees' experience, we have found it useful to ask the mentors and supervisors to comment on the changes (both positive and negative) they have observed as well.	**To what extent is the mentoring program contributing to the mentorees' career goals?**

Evaluation Criteria	What to Ask
Time and commitment Our research has shown that people benefit from the program in direct proportion to the time and effort they put in. It can be helpful to monitor the number of hours participants are dedicating to mentoring. In addition, while it is easy to focus on the mentoree's perception, consider getting feedback from the supervisor's point of view as well.	**How much time are participants spending on their mentoring activities and (more importantly) how satisfied are they with that amount of time?**
Suitability of mentoring matches The mid-point is a good time to check the vitality of the mentoring match. If you uncover unfavorable responses, consider discussing with the participants possible remedies they could use if either party feels their match is not working. Remind participants that closing down a partnership is not a failure. It may actually be a sign of growth in that the partners have outgrown the partnership and are ready to move on. Encourage the partners to celebrate their successes.	**How suitable are the mentoring matches?**

Evaluation Criteria	What to Ask
Participant effectiveness The mid-point written evaluation is both a product and a process. By asking participants to complete the evaluation, you are encouraging them to bring their accomplishments and learning outcomes to a conscious level.	**What is the mentor/mentoree doing well?** **What would you like to see the mentor/mentoree do more of?**
Program support Formal mentoring programs rely heavily on organizational support from supervisors, mentors and Program Coordinators. The program will need strong internal support throughout the entire process to sustain the mentoring partnerships.	**How supportive have the supervisors been? Program coordinators?** **How supportive was your mentor in preparing the Mentoring Action Plan?** **To what extent did you consult with the supervisor in the preparation of your mentoring plan?**
Strengths of the program & areas needing improvement Successful mentoring programs continually evaluate the development process and make quick adjustments to the program design if necessary.	**What parts of the mentoring program are working?** **What parts of the mentoring program are not working?**

MID-COURSE CORRECTION OR ADJUSTMENT

Once the data has been collected, it is important that "action" be taken when neccessary. For example, a mid-point evaluation found that the majority of the supervisors were unaware of the benefits of the program. They consistently responded unfavorably to survey items such as, "the program is worth the time investment required." Upon further investigation, the Program Coordinator discovered that the mentorees had not kept their supervisors informed about the program. Since the supervisors were not informed, they did not see individual progress, and questioned the overall benefits of the program. This important feedback led to a vital course correction. The Program Coordinator encouraged mentorees to have quarterly progress reviews with their supervisors.

END OF PROGRAM EVALUATION

The most important outcome of the end of program evaluation is to confirm that the program has positively impacted both the organization and its people. This evaluation should be designed to collect information that will assist the Program Coordinator in adjusting the overall program design, training and matching process. Data collected from the end of program is also beneficial in marketing and advertising as good anecdotal information tends to be revealed.

The following is a sample of the most common evaluation criteria:

Evaluation Criteria	What to Ask
Overall effectiveness The purpose of the end of program evaluation is to determine the degree to which the mentoring program benefited the individual participants.	**Overall, did the program offer participants a valuable experience?** **Was the program relevant to the employee's job?** **How effective were the developmental activities (feedback, learning forums, developmental assignments, etc.)?**
Organizational objectives A formal mentoring program also supports organizational objectives. Although organizational benefits are generally less dramatic than the individual benefits, real benefits to the organization do become apparent over time.	**What impact did the mentoring program have on various organizational goals and cultural changes?**

Evaluation Criteria	What to Ask
Matching process The end of program evaluation should be carefully constructed to determine what factors have had a positive (or negative) effect on the success of the mentoring match.	**Did differences in experience, age, personality style, and location have a positive or negative effect on the success of the partnership?**
Overall effectiveness of the mentoring relationship? Most evaluators want feedback from both the mentors and mentorees on their partner's effectiveness. This data is used to fine-tune future mentor/mentoree training programs.	**Were the mentors and mentorees effective in their roles?**
Program strengths & areas needing improvement Formal support tends to be comprehensive and includes a facilitated matching process, formal mentoring training and a variety of other program features. The end of program evaluation will want to uncover overall strengths as well as the areas needing improvement for future iterations.	**Did the program features effectively support the program outcomes?**

WHAT RESULTS WILL INDICATE SUCCESS?

A meaningful evaluation and tracking system is dependent upon how focused the program's purpose and goals were in the beginning. The evaluation process includes short-term measures, such as suitability of matches and time commitment. It also includes long-term measures, such as organizational benefits and the degree to which it helped participants achieve their goals. The following are clear indicators of success:

1) Mentoring is accepted as a valuable tool for leadership and career development throughout the organization.
2) Mentorees now recognize the skills they need for success in the areas of technical expertise, building relationships, and navigating the organization (political savvy).
3) Mentorees have discovered the developmental opportunities they need to enhance their skills.
4) Skills learned in the mentoring program are now applied on the job.
5) Mentorees have developed useful connections and partnerships.
6) Mentorees are taking responsibility for their own career development and are achieving realistic mentoring action plans.
7) Employees feel more committed to the organization.
8) Mentors and mentorees now recommend the program

to peers and colleagues.

9) Mentorees return as mentors.
10) Employee morale and quality of work life have improved.
11) A future pool of competent leaders has been created.

HOW TO COLLECT THE DATA

Feedback can be collected using a variety of mechanisms, such as on-line assessment tools, personal interviews and focus groups. In addition, more subtle indicators to gauge the effectiveness of the mentoring program can include a) attendance of mentors and mentorees at various training events together, b) the degree of progress the mentorees are making on their mentoring plans, and c) casual comments and anecdotes the participants offer.

While evaluation is the last step in the mentoring process, its success is entirely dependent upon how well the program was planned up front. The program purpose and goals must be clearly defined so they can be measured, evaluated and improved when necessary. An effective evaluation system must define what success looks like, and at the same time, demonstrate that investing in human resource development is worth the time and effort it requires.

PRACTICAL EXAMPLES AND TECHNIQUES

Establish a Tracking System

Establish an effective tracking system that ensures continual improvement of the program. Be sure to measure the benefits of the mentoring program to the organization, its mentors and its mentorees.

Questions to Consider:

- How will the Mentoring Design Team track the success of the mentoring program?
- What results will indicate success?
- How will the Mentoring Design Team collect and evaluate the data?
- What will the Mentoring Design Team do with the results?

NOTES

Conclusion

IN CLOSING...

Successful organizations are revolutionizing the way they are developing their employees. They are moving away from traditional training approaches that rely on formal classroom training alone and are creating conditions where learning happens continuously through a variety of developmental experiences and mentoring partnerships.

To effectively develop employees, remember ***The Keys to Mentoring Success:***

1) Make individual learning relevant to organizational goals.
2) Build support at all levels.
3) Create a comprehensive and systematic matching process.
4) Prepare the people involved by providing training on roles and responsibilities.
5) Provide a wide range of learning experiences and activities.
6) Use technology to manage the administrative details of formal mentoring partnerships.
7) Evaluate and fine-tune often.

Bibliography: Mentoring and Career Development Resources

Bell, C. *Managers as Mentors.* San Francisco: Barrett-Koehler Publishers, 1996.

Bolton, R., and Bolton, D. *People Styles at Work.* New York: AMACOM, 1996.

Buckingham, M., and Clifton, D. *Now, Discover Your Strengths.* New York: The Free Press, 2001.

Bedrosian, M. *Speak Like A Pro.* New York: John Wiley and Sons, Inc., 1987.

Bridges, W. *Creating You & Co.* Reading: Addison-Wesley, 1997.

Blanchard, Shula. *Everyone's a Coach.* New York: Harper Business, 1995.

Bonnstetter, Suiter, Widrick. *The Universal Language, DISC.* Scottsdale: Target Training International, Inc., 1995.

Clutterbuck, D., (February 2002). *Why Mentoring Programs and Relationships Fail.* Link and Learn (Online).

Dalton, M. and Hollenbeck G. *How to Design an Effective System for Developing Managers and Leaders.* Greensboro, NC: Center for Creative Leadership, 1996.

Drahosz, K and Rhodes, D. *Dynamic Mentoring,* Montclair: The Training Connection, 1997.

Drahosz, K. *Dynamic Mentoring: An Orientation Guide,* Montclair: The Training Connection, 1999.

Drahosz, K. *Dynamic Mentoring: Mid Point Energizer.* Montclair: The Training Connection, 1999.

Farren, C. *Who's Running Your Career?* Austin: Bard Press, 1997.

Goldsmith, M., Kay, B., and Shelton, S. *Learning Journeys.* Palo Alto: Davies-Black Publishing, 2000.

Goleman, D. *Working with Emotional Intelligence.* New York: Bantam Book, 1998.

Jossi, F. *Mentoring in Changing Times.* Training, 50-54, 1997, August.

Kouzes, J., and Posner, B. *Credibility.* San Franciso: Jossey-Bass, 1993.

Krannich, R. *Change Your Job Change Your Life.* Manassas Park: Impact Publications, 1994.

Leeds, D. *Smart Questions.* New York: McGraw-Hill Book Company, 1987.

Mayer, J. *Find the Job You've Always Wanted in Half the Time with Half the Effort.* Chicago: Contemporary Books Inc., 1992.

McCall, M., Lombardo, M. and Morrison, A. *The Lessons of Experience.* New York: The Free Press, 1988.

Murray, M. and Owen, M. *Beyond the Myths and Magic of Mentoring: How to Facilitate an Effective Mentoring Program.* San Francisco: Jossey-Bass, 2000.

Neff, J., and Citrin, J. *Lessons from the Top.* New York: Currency Doubleday, 1999.

Neuhauser, Peg. *Corporate Legends & Lore.* New York: Warner Books, 1993.

Northup, Jan. *What Makes the Difference: Success Strategies for The Promotable Woman.* Springfield: PRW Partnership, 1988.

Parks, Daloz Sharon. *Big Questions, Worthy Dreams.* San Francisco: Jossey-Bass, 2000.

Porter, S., Porter K., and Bennett, C. *Me, Myself, & I, Inc.* Manassas Park: Impact Publications, 1998.

Waterman, R., Waterman, J., and Collard, B. *Toward a Career-Resiliant Workforce.* Harvard Business Review, 1994.

Wendleton, K. *Job-Search Secrets.* New York: The Five O'clock Books, 1997.

Wickman, F., and Sjodin, T. Mentoring: *A Success Guide for Mentors and Proteges.* New York: McGraw-Hill, 1997.

Wicks, Robert. *Sharing Wisdom.* New York: The Crossroad Publishing Company, 2000.

Zemke, R., Raines, C., and Filipczak, B. *Generations at Work.* New York: AMACOM, 2000.

A

The Mentoring Connection: An Innovative Mentoring Tool

THE MENTORING CONNECTION

Harnessing the power of internet to manage formal mentoring programs.

Introducing The Mentoring Connection (TMC)

TMC is a web-based delivery system that was developed to offer business, government and non-profit organizations a comprehensive, effective and efficient means of establishing and operating formal mentoring programs and partnerships.

Through the use of sophisticated data management tools, **TMC** can streamline administrative and processing operations while maintaining the personal aspects so critical to effective mentoring programs.

Mentoring Programs Without the Hassle

Whether you have an established mentoring program, or are just launching a new one, **The Mentoring Connection** can offer the following enhancements to your program:

- ***Quicker implementation of a formalized mentoring program.*** Mentors and mentorees apply to the mentoring program on-line by completing an application form that includes a biographical profile. **TMC** collects this important data to make selections, facilitate future matches and track the relationship after these matches have been made.

- ***Easier, more effective matching of mentors and mentorees.*** The success of a formal mentoring program is dependent upon a carefully orchestrated selection and matching process. There are a variety of ways to match participants. These methods range from formal matches by an outside committee/task force to a more informal one that encompasses one's own mentoring philosophy. **TMC** assists organizations in matching mentors with mentorees by collecting vital information and then employing a dynamic scoring system to match mentorees with an appropriate mentor. Every effort is made to match mentorees with someone who can best support their developmental needs.

- ***Insightful self and 360 degree feedback.*** Most mentoring programs begin with developmental feedback. Confidential self and multi-rater feedback provides employees an opportunity to target developmental needs and goals and in turn develop effective learning plans. **TMC** supports two popular assessment tools: The Success Triangle© (a multi-rater feedback system) and Managing for Success® (a DISC self assessment). More information on these tools can be found in Appendices B and C respectively.

- ***Less hands-on administration and processing.*** An on-line Mentoring Action Plan and Mentoring

Agreement provides a roadmap for keeping partnerships on track and on target. The plans are based on an individual assessment of the mentorees' needs and are supported by adequate resources and an active mentoring partnership. The Program Coordinator can use this feature to forecast funding requirements as well as to analyze the collective training needs of the mentoring group.

- ***Communication between the Program Coordinator and mentoring participants.*** An on-line forum for mentors, mentorees and the Program Coordinator provides the tool they need to stay connected through a threaded discussion style bulletin board.

- ***Efficient online scheduling of mentoring activities.*** An on-line calendar of events provides the Program Coordinator an opportunity to post upcoming events and developmental opportunities.

- ***Program evaluations that keep you on top of progress and problems.*** Continual evaluation of the development process is an integral part of a successful mentoring program. Consistent monitoring will ensure that pro-active adjustments are made to the program design to facilitate further success. **TMC** provides an on-line evaluation process that collects information that clearly determines what aspects of the program are successful and what areas could benefit from a course correction or adjustment.

- ***More efficient collection and storage of data and resource materials.*** **TMC** offers an on-line newsletter highlighting mentoring success stories and lessons learned. In addition, **TMC** has a Library where the Program Coordinator can post Articles, Workbooks, PowerPoint Presentations and other key resource materials that offer mentoring tips and techniques.

- ***Accessible, secure and complete privacy for all information.*** **TMC** provides the infrastructure, including hardware, software, data-encryption certification through Verisign (to protect personal information), and high-speed connectivity. **TMC** has been verified to meet all *U.S. Section 508 Guidelines* of the Rehabilitation Act.

If you are interested in learning more about **TMC,** please contact **The Training Connection, Inc.** at (703) 551-0734 for a complimentary demo.

APPENDIX A: THE MENTORING CONNECTION

B

The Success Triangle: Success through Feedback

WHAT DOES SUCCESS LOOK LIKE?

The Training Connection, Inc. (TTC) has spent the last 10 years researching, observing and predicting success in today's workplace and has found that successful employees have three things in common: 1) they are recognized and appreciated for their technical expertise, 2) they possess good relationship skills and 3) they understand how to navigate the organization's formal and informal structures.

A process used to evaluate one's own success (as perceived through the eyes of others) has become known as 360 degree or multi-rater feedback. Multi-rater feedback provides a comprehensive view of a person's behavior from a circle of contacts, who are in many cases, closer to the action.

The Success Triangle©

Feedback provided through a popular 360 degree tool known as The Success Triangle (Drahosz and Rhodes, 1997) is a reliable source for a person's performance data. The ultimate goal of The Success Triangle is to help employees understand the skills and behaviors that impact their success on the job. The Success Triangle is organized into three-skill clusters:

Expertise - how effective an individual is at mastering the expertise required of their job or career field.

Building relationships - how effective the individual is at building relationships and connections with others.

Navigating the organization - how effective the individual is at understanding and navigating the organization through its formal and informal structures.

Participants receive an assessment designed to identify developmental opportunities in 13 skill clusters. Each Success Triangle includes nine on-line surveys. One survey is completed by the employee, one is completed by his or her immediate supervisor, and the remaining seven surveys are completed by a combination of the employee's superiors, peers and direct reports. An outside coach will administer the assessment, track and collect the results for processing and provide one-on-one confidential feedback sessions.

THINGS TO KEEP IN MIND WHEN WORKING WITH 360 DEGREE FEEDBACK:

- **Focus on Both Strengths and Weaknesses.** The value of feedback is that it gives employees an opportunity to build on strengths and develop strategies for overcoming weaknesses.

- **Uncover Significant Themes, Patterns and Trends.** Look for overarching themes. Has anyone ever given similar feedback? Pay careful attention to redundancy.

- **Feedback is Neither Right nor Wrong.** Feedback is simply another view of how a person's actions impact others. By understanding how actions and behaviors impact others, the employee is better prepared to evaluate whether being perceived this way makes them more or less effective in their job.

- **Developmental Purposes Only.** The Success Triangle is used for developmental purposes only. When employees know that the results of their feedback will not be used for appraisals, selections or promotions, a new and candid avenue for communication is opened for everyone involved. Information gained using The Success Triangle enhances confidence, is non-threatening and absolutely confidential.

If you are interested in learning more about The Success Triangle, please contact **The Training Connection, Inc.** at (703) 551-0734 for a complimentary demo.

C

More about DISC: Embracing Differences

HOW TO CREATE HARMONY IN A MENTORING RELATIONSHIP

An Introduction to DISC

Any successful mentoring relationship can be compared to a good orchestra. Individuals who bear little resemblance to each other often need to learn how to harmonize and respect the differences they bring to the relationship. Their diversity in style and substance, when properly harmonized, can create a great score.

It is rather easy for a conductor to identify who plays what instrument and it is no less important for mentors to know the behavioral styles of the individuals they mentor. These attributes can be determined in a non-threatening environment and can help to launch mentorees and mentors on a voyage of personal discovery.

For many years, successful mentoring programs have relied upon a tool called **DISC** to identify behavioral styles. **DISC** describes the four basic elements of human behavior as: **D**ominance, **I**nfluence, **S**teadiness and **C**ompliance. The basis for this assessment tool began as early as 400BC, when Hippocrates observed clear and consistent similarities and differences in the way people interact. We still rely upon observable behavior to better understand and enhance our own relationships.

DISC Defined

DISC is a universal language that explains behavior and emotions and is based on factors that transcend gender, race and culture. Its premise is that all people exhibit all four **DISC** styles to one degree or another, regardless of their background and experience.

The key to **DISC** is discovering the degree of intensity a person brings to these four areas of behavior:

> ***Dominance:*** How one approaches problems and challenges.
> ***Influence:*** How one interacts and influences people.
> ***Steadiness:*** How one responds to change and levels of activity.
> ***Compliance:*** How one responds to rules and regulations.

The Dominance factor, for example, does not measure whether or not a person can solve problems, but rather measures how the person goes about solving problems and challenges. Once an individual has developed a heightened awareness of their **DISC** style, they can begin to consciously control their behavior and communication style. For example, if someone is the type of person who is stressed by tight deadlines they might take extra care to timeline complex projects. Conversely, if an individual is dealing with a manager who is very "bottom-line" oriented they will want to come to a meeting prepared to talk results and stick to business.

Embracing Differences

It barely suffices to know the differences in people's styles unless effective partnerships are built. This requires ongoing commitment from mentors and mentorees, and although a good mentoring connection between two people may "just happen," relationships are generally built over time and must include a mutual respect that is based on trust and transcends differences. **DISC** is a valuable aid to help people better understand themselves and others. Awareness of this process will help to avoid conflicts and enhance the mentoring relationship.

Why do people act the way they do? Why do priorities differ from person to person? Why does it seem so hard to approach some people while others seem to mirror your values, attitudes and interests?

Differences in work styles quickly become obvious in a mentoring relationship. One individual may pay considerable attention to quality and detail while another is more of a "big picture" thinker.

Fortunately, it is possible to observe and predict these types of differences and how they might "show up" in a mentoring relationship. Knowledge of different work and behavioral types, in itself, helps mentoring pairs to adapt their styles to compliment those of their partner. **DISC** has a long history of achieving these kinds of goals in many different mentoring environments.

The Benefits

DISC helps mentors and mentorees to:

- Develop long-term mentoring relationships.
- Communicate more effectively.
- Establish goals that benefit individuals and organizations.
- Establish realistic milestones for performance and skills enhancement.
- Identify obstacles and problem areas that may be adversely affecting progress.
- Generate alternatives and action plans to overcome problems.

The **DISC** process can provide mentoring partnerships from different functions and areas within an organization the opportunity to meet, learn about each other and learn more about how to build important working relationships throughout the organization.

If you are interested in learning more about your **DISC** behavioral style, please visit

http://www.thetrainingconnection.com/styleform.htm

or call **The Training Connection, Inc.** at (703) 551-0734.

About the Author

KATHY WENTWORTH DRAHOSZ

Kathy Wentworth Drahosz, founder and President of **The Training Connection, Inc.,** brings more than twenty years of experience in business, product and people development. As a Certified Professional Behavioral Analyst (CPBA) Kathy has helped thousands of individuals worldwide experience the power of her training programs and services.

A strong focus of Kathy's work has been in helping businesses and other organizations develop effective, formal mentoring programs.

In addition to personally presenting numerous training programs in the mentoring field, Kathy is the co-developer and author of *Dynamic Mentoring, Mentoring for Success* and *Discovering the Mentor Within,* three practical approaches to unleashing human potential.

A recent endeavor has been the development of "The Mentoring Connection," a new and innovative, web-based delivery system developed to offer businesses and other organizations a comprehensive, effective and cost-efficient means of establishing and operating formal mentoring programs and partnerships. Through the use of the Internet and sophisticated data management tools, this program makes effective mentoring programs possible with significant savings in staff and administrative overhead.

The list of clients of **The Training Connection, Inc.** represents many of the leading business and government agencies across the country. Kathy has designed, developed and implemented long-range mentoring programs for the Department of Energy, Defense Threat Reduction Agency, Department of State, Library of Congress, International Broadcasting Bureau, Maryland-National Capital Park and Planning Commission, Bureau of Economic Analysis, Patent and Trademark Office, US Customs Service, Veterans Affairs, Veterans Benefits Administration, Veterans Health Administration, NASA, EPA, Department of Education, Department of Health and Human Services, Loudoun County Social Services and Prince William County's Welfare to Work Programs. A number of private organizations have benefited from her programs including Emerson Motors, BayAlarm Security Company, Booz Allen Hamilton, BAE and Tech Corp.

A NOTE TO THE READER...

Although the benefits of mentoring to organizations are too numerous to count, true mentoring success can only be measured through personal fulfillment and the knowledge that you made a difference. By taking the time to create a mentoring process that develops people, you have impacted not only the success of individuals in the workplace but also the success of the organization.

Thank you for your commitment to helping people and organizations grow!

Kathy
Kathy Wentworth Drahosz

Keys to Mentoring Success Index